EBUR
BECOMI

Michelle Mendonça Bambawale wears many hats—professional educator, passionate photographer, aspiring environmentalist, amateur gardener, wannabe ambassador for world peace and now, writer.

Having spent a happy childhood in a Goan Catholic family in Pune, India, she has lived around the world raising her own nomadic family.

Michelle has been writing for as long as she can remember, from inventing plays in primary school to writing scripts in college. As a young professional, she contributed to the *Times of India*, Young Mother, *Femina* and A&M (Advertising and Marketing) in India, and to the *Khaleej Times* and *Gulf News* in the UAE.

Michelle began blogging in 2008 and *Becoming Goan* is her first book.

Celebrating 35 Years of
Penguin Random House India

ADVANCE PRAISE FOR THE BOOK

'Michelle Bambawale's book is a touching Goan story with a universal appeal—a story of identity, culture and belonging. The idea of Goa is where new India meets the old, and Michelle weaves her storytelling skills with empathy and a human touch. It's a story that is wistful and vivid in its description of a unique land. [Read this book] to discover the essence of Goa [and] embark on a journey to know what it means to be Goan!'

—Rajdeep Sardesai, consulting editor, India Today TV

BECOMING
Goan

A contemporary coming-home story

Michelle
Mendonça Bambawale

EBURY
PRESS

An imprint of Penguin Random House

EBURY PRESS

USA | Canada | UK | Ireland | Australia
New Zealand | India | South Africa | China | Singapore

Ebury Press is part of the Penguin Random House group of companies
whose addresses can be found at global.penguinrandomhouse.com

Published by Penguin Random House India Pvt. Ltd
4th Floor, Capital Tower 1, MG Road,
Gurugram 122 002, Haryana, India

First published in Ebury Press by Penguin Random House India 2023

ISBN 9780143462361

For sale in the Indian Subcontinent only

Typeset in Sabon by Manipal Technologies Limited, Manipal
Printed at Thomson Press India Ltd, New Delhi

www.penguin.co.in

Contents

Who Am I? A Real Goan or a Pandemic Migrant?

Casa Mendonça in 2020

Late on 20 June 2020, my family and I received our government permit online to drive from Mumbai to Goa. We packed overnight and left early the next morning, nervous about the drive under uncomfortable and unfamiliar

1

circumstances. During the Covid-19 lockdown, we were
stuck in our flat in Bandra, Mumbai for the first three
months. We were now driving to the home I had inherited
in Siolim, North Goa, as we needed to get there urgently to
manage our house during the brutal Goan monsoons. What
we didn't know then was that this was going to be a long-
term relocation for our nomadic family.

I was born in Poona (now Pune) in 1966, in a Goan
Catholic home, and was named Michelle by my godfather
after the popular Beatles song. I lived in Pune for twenty
years, which is the longest I have lived in any place, so far.
Growing up, most summers, I holidayed in Siolim and visited
each of my four grandparents' houses in Goa. In 1986, I
moved to Bombay (now Mumbai) to study and then work.
In February 1988, I joined the advertising agency Ogilvy, a
move that would forever change my life. I met Bharat, an
ambitious, bright man with deep dimples and a determined
gait. We fell in love on a train ride back home to Pune. After
getting married in 1989, we lived in Mumbai for a few years.
Our son Kunal was born in 1991. Bharat's career took the
three of us to Dubai, UAE, in 1993, where we began our
expat life. In 1995, we welcomed our daughter, Divya.

After ten years in Dubai, Bharat's expanded
responsibilities and geography took our family to Bangkok,
Thailand, and five years later, to London, England.
We returned to India, to Delhi in 2011, with a plan to
reacclimatize to living and working in India, before retiring
in Goa. We got closer to it by moving to Mumbai in 2016.
It was Covid-19 that propelled the four of us and our
Labrador, Haruki, to relocate to Goa in June 2020. I was
looking to find safety in a place my grandparents had left.

Both my grandfathers, Jerry (Jerome/Jeronimo) Mendonça and Marshall D'Lima left Goa around the early 1900s for high school, to study in English in British India. My grandmothers Lulu Tavares and Eslinda Vaz, despite their abilities and motivations, could not study beyond middle school as education in Goan villages for girls was limited and only in Portuguese. Grandma Eslinda would insist: 'I want my daughters and granddaughters to study hard and get degrees. I taught myself English and Hindi.'

My grandfathers went on to work for the British Raj— Jerry Mendonça for the railways and Marshall D'Lima for the post and telegraphs. Both had transferable jobs and travelled the length and breadth of the country, helping build two critical elements of India's infrastructure. They wore sola topis, played tennis and retired in bucolic Poona to live in rented flats— the Mendonça grandparents in 1946 and the D'Limas in 1952. For them, English was a ticket to a better life and so, they did not teach their children any Konkani. Neither of my parents—Albert Mendonça and Bridget (Biddie) D'Lima Mendonça—were born in Goa, nor did they know any Konkani to teach us. Tragic, as language is the key to a culture.

I had always had a complicated relationship with my Goan lineage. I had never lived in Goa full-time and I did not speak Konkani. I knew little of this land, its many histories and mysteries, and was the clichéd global citizen. The design of my home in Siolim is a metaphor for my life here—while the centre and the heart remain Goan, the extension has a modern, multicultural dimension.

My grandfather Jerry's grandfather, also named Jeronimo Mendonça, built this house in 1859. It still stands solid at the centre and remains the soul of our home. In line with our plan to one day retire in Goa, we added an extension to the original house while living in Bangkok and London. It was completed and christened Casa Mendonça in 2009. The extension has contemporary comforts but retains the high Goan ceilings typical of the original house. Additionally, we swapped the *balcao*,* for a Thai-style pergola, since Bangkok had been our favourite place to live. We worked collaboratively with a talented, young Goan architect—Amit Sukhthankar. His blueprint with its open indoor-outdoor plan captured who we are. Everyone who visits gushes about its genealogy—'So special to live in this home that has been in your family for generations. It is so warm and welcoming.' We decorated the house with a handful of family heirlooms as well as our eclectic collection of books, photos, art, furniture and junk from our lives and travels across the country and the world.

I have some gorgeous black and white family photos and my grandfather Jerry Mendonça's diary. It records familial births, marriages, deaths, and details of the original house with a coconut grove and paddy fields. His entry on 16 May 1947 mentions: 'This testament says that payment must be made to offer low masses in the month of October, every year till the world exists, therefore must not be forgotten as a law of God.' It goes on: 'First for the souls of grandfather Jeronimo Mendonça and grandmother, Maria Sebastina Sequeira, second for all the souls of the house, third for all the souls in need

---

* Portuguese for front porch or patio. Typical for traditional Goan houses.

and fourth for all the souls in purgatory. These masses may be said in Goa or out of Goa.' He has written and signed it in his calligraphic handwriting in Portuguese and English. The paper is now parchment, the black ink blurring, blotting and fading.

My dad's second sister, Aunty Bertha, was born here on 27 May 1921. After Casa Mendonça was ready in 2009, she was always keen to walk visitors around and show them the bed and the room where she was born. Of the five Mendonça siblings, only she and Aunty Sylvie (Sister Maryann) survived to experience this extension. It was devastating for me to go through the torturous building process remotely without Daddy. He was a civil engineer and loved supervising construction sites. Thrilled with the early drawings, he had scrutinized the plans closely. Tragically, before the work started, Daddy passed away on 5 June 2006. Fortunately, both of Bharat's parents, Aai and Baba, were our pillars through the traumatic building process and loved visiting Siolim. As Baba aged, he refused to travel anywhere other than Casa Mendonça.

During one of their visits from Pune in May 2011, when Aunty Bertha was turning ninety, Aai, over breakfast, enthused, 'I dreamt that there are gold coins buried under this big cross in the front of the house.' I put down my cup of coffee and was ready to start digging; we could use some gold to pay for the escalating costs. I knew that a small gold cross is usually blessed and buried, similar to a *bhoomi* puja, where you pray to Mother Earth to bless the foundation, the construction and the home. My sister Ingrid, Aunty Bertha and our neighbour Maria with the parish priest had blessed this new construction, which

A recent photo of our crazy Lab, Haruki, and the cross
in the front of the house: Is Haruki praying for
forgiveness for his many transgressions?

included burying the tiny gold cross. I wondered if the
tradition extended to burying gold coins under the cross in
front of the house. That morning, over breakfast, as Aunty
Bertha dipped her pao into her steaming cup of tea, she
responded, 'I don't think there are any gold coins under the
cross. But once, when we were sitting and stitching here,
over our summer holidays, we needed to find needles and
thread. My mother started rummaging around in that niche,
[she pointed to the cupboard in the wall behind her]. She
spotted something shiny tucked at the back of the drawer
and when she tugged, a handful of gold sovereigns fell out.'
Aai, Baba and I stopped eating our morning pao with Amul
butter and looked up and said, 'Where? That wall? In this
room?' They had once found a solid gold treasure right
where we were sitting.

Over the years, coming to this house has given me a sense of belonging, I feel a connection to a culture that was familiar, yet alien.

In India, people always want to know, 'But where is your native place?' 'Where are you from?' In work situations, this question is usually a superficial icebreaker or, in social situations, cocktail party conversations. I stumble and stammer: 'I lived in Pune till I was twenty, so that should make me Maharashtrian, but most Indians identify as Malayali, Bengali, Punjabi and Gujarati even if they have never lived in any of those states. I guess that's how this works. So going by ancestry, I'm Goan.'

In contemporary Goa, when I answer the same question, it is met with wonder, 'You are from here? A real Goan? A local?' Goa enthusiasts and Goaphiles have often asked me about my Portuguese ancestry, my Portuguese house and if my parents or grandparents spoke Portuguese. I have no Portuguese history. My roots are Goan.

The labels I struggle with are: Goan, local, Portuguese, migrant, outsider and foreigner. I wonder what they mean to me.

The Covid-19 timeout allowed me to reflect on my Goan identity. I felt that it was time to write my reflections on this lived paradox—a look at Goa from the outside, as well as a journey of discovery. In this book, I try to unpack complex anthropological theories of identity and culture based on my search for my Goan roots. I accept that these are constantly developing, and I interpret and wear them as they suit my selfish agenda.

After eighteen years of living as an expat and looking in from the outside of the host country, I now find myself in a strange position living in Goa. I wonder if I am an insider, given my Goan heritage. As an expat, you know your stay is temporary and that you are always an outsider. I now find myself torn between two worlds—the Goan and the outsider, but I don't belong in either. I guess we all suffer from some incarnation of the impostor syndrome.

Turbulent Covid-19 times made me question—Is the pursuit of happiness to find love, home, family and safety? Is home a place or a people? I pondered existential questions of being and belonging with Goa as my focus: sitting in my pergola, looking out on my tropical garden with centuries-old mango and tamarind trees, my three crazy dogs at my feet, exotic birds singing loudly, bees pollinating flowers and huge, multicoloured butterflies swooping all around me. A feeling of home. A connection to this red earth.

Courtesy: Karan Khosla

A family photo taken in October 2020 under the benevolent mango tree

My relocation to Goa realigned my priorities, transforming me from an international person of mystery to a child of the soil, a village Goan. Instead of the

Guardian and the *New York Times,* I read *O'Heraldo* and *Navhind Times.** I focused my learning on Goan issues. I no longer philosophized about improving educational learning outcomes but the cashew crop instead. As I became parochial, I got varying reactions from my family and friends. They looked sceptical when I complained about how burgeoning construction was choking Goa, its rich culture and biodiversity, or when I said, 'Goa's very own Mancurad and Manghilar† mangoes are the true Queens, much sweeter and better than the King—Alphonso.' My obsession with Goan issues was so complete that friends and family teased me about 'going native'.

Still, others provoked, 'Are you sure you are a real Goan? You don't look or sound Goan,' further compounding my mounting self-doubt. I didn't know what that meant, so I shrugged. I did not speed on a motorbike or have a mohawk or man bun. Was that how Goans looked?

Living here, I met 'outsiders', 'residents' and 'settlers' who had moved to Goa or owned second and third homes here. They included me as their token authentic Goan friend and did not seem to know any other Goans in their local social circle. Everyone else was another settler or outsider. I wondered if it was representative of the times we live in. In India, they are called reservations. You get a seat at the table—on the board or in school if you tick a box. The one woman, or better still, the minority person of colour. Here, did I tick three boxes: Goan, Catholic, woman?

---

* Local newspapers.
† Types of Goan mangoes.

Serendipitously, my Goan family, friends and neighbours took me on as a project and aimed to mentor me in embracing the culture and traditions. They probably shook their heads and rolled their eyes at how little I knew.

Over the last few years, Bharat and I have done freelance consultancy work in marketing and education respectively, that allows us to not go into a physical workplace five days a week but remain engaged with our professions. Enough to keep our minds stretched, our mouths fed and our souls not sucked out. When we tried to work from Goa pre-Covid, professional associates did not take us seriously. They chortled, 'You are in Goa, have a great time, party on, come back and we will talk.' No one believed we could work from anywhere but Covid allowed us to live in and work from Siolim.

The pandemic changed the Goa narrative. A little. The working from home (WFH) acronym became working from Goa (WFG). Not just hippies, foreigners and migrants, but middle-class, urban Indians started to look at it as a place to live. Others invested in Goa for when they needed a getaway. Some moved with suitcases of cash, a fleet of fancy cars and a retinue of staff (that would make the Granthams of *Downton Abbey* envious) while some rocked up with their seven dogs in an old Maruti van. There were others who got onto a plane with their laptop, business plans and dreams, or a bus with their backpack and books. An old friend, Sameena, recently told me, 'We got stranded here during the lockdown and now love it: the beaches, bars, live music, fun neighbours, so different from Pune. I am never going back.'

Post-lockdown hordes headed for Goa

Glossy lifestyle, travel and architectural magazines splash spreads about the best and newest spots in Goa ever since Covid began. Whenever these lists are released, my phone blows up with messages, 'Have you tried this new place yet?' Every hour, social media influencers update their posts, stories, shorts and reels with a stunning view, an offbeat adventure, an outstanding restaurant or their top five tips. Everyone was in Goa or wished they were in Goa. #GoaFOMO (fear of missing out) was real and everything Goa and Goan was a trending hashtag.

Discerning tourists also started looking beyond the tired party stereotype. They wanted the history, the culture, the food, the genuine Goan or Portuguese experience. Visitors would insist: 'We don't want the usual beachy stuff. We are looking for real, local, experiences. We want the unexplored Goa.' Handpicked. Curated. Hidden gems. Village walks, birding trails, heritage houses. 'Live like a local, eat like a local' were terms I often heard. I wondered, was I a local now? Was I living the authentic Goan village life?

Pre-pandemic when I was asked 'Where do you live in Goa?' I would say 'Siolim'. Then quickly qualify with 'it's a village in North Goa'. If there was no recognition, I would carry on, 'It's further north from the Calangute–Candolim beaches. Close to Anjuna and Vagator. You need to cross the bridge in Siolim to get to the beaches of Morjim, Ashwem and Arambol.'

Since the pandemic, the calls and messages go like this: 'We are staying in Siolim in this incredible hotel.' 'We are in this Airbnb in Siolim.' 'We bought a flat in Siolim.' 'We are renting this amazing villa with a pool in Siolim.' 'We just love living in Siolim, man. So many fab coworking cafes and restaurants.' 'I have just moved to Siolim, around the corner from you.' Or: 'Did you buy, build or inherit in Siolim, or are you from here?'

I feel we are at a tipping point of Goan identity and culture in Siolim and in the North, where Covid has accelerated the appeal and brought rapid-fire development.

It is now time to tell my own 'finding Siolim' story. In this book, I reminisce and reflect on myself, my village, my community and Goan rural life over the past few years.

I struggle with the vulnerability of writing a memoir and the responsibility of documenting Siolim and Goa today. I am consumed by the notion of writing my coming home to

Goa story. I have to tell my truth—I have abstained from writing about food (including family recipes), music and architecture, as those are our favourite tropes, but I know little about them. Academics, historians, poets and writers may cringe. My storytelling is based on strong emotions, romantic memories, sweeping generalizations and shameless eavesdropping. I may also have some propensity for exaggeration and sarcasm. Conversations and characters have been created for effect.

Will the Goan Identity Survive in Contemporary Goa?

The phone rings, again. A former colleague, Amar, from Delhi, begins: 'We want to move to Goa and are looking for a Portuguese house. Our friends are also looking.' He tells me the quality of life is the draw—the emerald cover and the fresh sea breeze. Then there is the vibe—the creative space, *susegad** life, the charm of Portuguese houses. I wonder if they believe that living in villages in the north of Goa is the same as living in the south of Europe. I ask, 'Where are these Portuguese houses? There are Goan houses. The Portuguese did not live in these villages; they lived mainly in the towns and cities. Goans built these houses on their land with their hard-earned money using Indo-Portuguese architectural influences.' He is not convinced. He messages me brochures and newspaper advertisements selling 'Portuguese houses' and asks if I have the time to go and check them out.

---

* Comes from the Portuguese word 'sossegado' which means quiet and calm. It is about Goa's relaxed, laid-back attitude to life.

Morning walks down the road

I also hear from Goans looking to sell—the Goan diaspora (Goans living in other cities and countries) with no intention of ever living here. They prefer the big city life with contemporary cultures and conveniences. They rant, 'You have lived in London and Mumbai; why would you choose to live in a village, so narrow-minded? No decent public transport. So much corruption. Nothing interesting ever happens. Everyone in your business, gossiping and telling you what to do and not do.' They cannot deal with Goa today but have great *saudade** for their homeland. A

---

* Portuguese word for a feeling of longing, melancholy or nostalgia.

friend in Oz enthuses, 'It was so much fun spending summer holidays in my grandparents' immense house in Saligao. They had so many mango and jackfruit trees that we loved climbing. Cleaning that *ponnos** was messy, but so yummy. My grandmother used to cook fish curry for us on a wood fire, that great Nistyachem koddi[†] with the smoky flavour and the next morning our breakfast was kalchikodi[‡] wiping up the kunli[§] with poi. I miss that special taste of Goa.' Uncle Cyril from Canada smiles on our family Zoom call and says: 'We chased pigs and jumped in springs and wells for a swim. Sometimes we went crabbing on full moon nights. Every evening we would all sit on the balcao and say the rosary.' He is nostalgic about evenings spent watching the sunset on Goan beaches or balcaos, guitars and fenis in hand . . . They believe Goa is paradise lost and that the Goan spirit is being diluted. (Figuratively, not literally, thankfully.)

We listen to Goans living here struggling to manage and maintain their ancestral houses and land--paying rising bills, suffocating with overcrowding on the streets, shortages and escalating prices of basics, exorbitant fencing costs to keep out stray dogs and cows, trying to get *Krishi*, farmer status and drowning in paperwork to get water rebates for agricultural land. Aunty Ruth is exasperated: 'The electricity is always going. It is so hot without the fan. We are getting old, no; we can't manage this big house and garden. Only two of us left here. Those monkeys are

---

* Konkani for jackfruit.
[†] Konkani for fish curry rice.
[‡] Konkani for yesterday's curry.
[§] Konkani for the mud cooking pot.

always breaking the Mangalore tiles on the roof. Cows are trying to eat our plants. Tourists are making our Goa so dirty, throwing water and beer bottles into our property. So much traffic, can't walk on the roads. Fish has become so expensive. How to manage now, my girl?' They want to sell their ancestral homes and land. Older folk who felt isolated over the pandemic are moving in with their families in other cities or countries, or into senior living options. Many have Portuguese passports and are waiting to relocate there. (Fun fact: If you, your parents or grandparents were born in Goa before 1961, you are eligible for Portuguese citizenship).

In Goa, the current amalgamation of cultures is moving from Goan and Portuguese to Bollywood on one hand and globalized capitalism on the other. You can hear loud bhangra beats in shacks, dished up with generous helpings of chicken tikka and served with a side of mutter paneer. When you land in Goa, both airports welcome you with a giant Starbucks (terrible, expensive coffee). Food outlets such as McDonald's, Pizza Hut, KFC, Taco Bell and Burger King have found their way here and are gaining popularity. Everything across the world is now same, same. What you eat, what you shop, how you dress. We are all slaves to conformity. That essential Goan essence is disappearing.

My stomach clenches and I feel the bile build up when I see male tourists tumbling out of buses in search of cold beer, butter chicken and female flesh. I have witnessed the golden North Goa beach belt cannibalized. Young and not-so-young guys with a leer in their eyes head in packs for the beach. Historically, with the influx of hippies since the 1970s, one of Goa's attractions has been to catch a glimpse of bikini-clad women. This trend persists.

Goans struggle emotionally with the influx of migrants that cuts across the economic and social class—from the labourer working on a construction site, in the fields or on coconut plantations, in a home, hotel or floating casino or as a security guard, to the more affluent looking to buy a flat, a house, a second or third home, a restaurant, or a piece of Goa as well as the many evolving avatars of the quintessential hippies colonizing Goa since the 1970s.

During the pandemic, beyond everyone being a Covid expert, there was also a vast community of Goa experts. I met many friends, friends of friends and acquaintances who were tourists, Covid migrants, nomads and settlers— all could be identified as wannabe Goans, Goaphiles, Goa enthusiasts, Goans at heart, etc. They made sure they mansplained many things about Goa and being Goan. If I knew little, they knew much less, but that did not stop them from being an authority on not just quarantine times and vaccines, but food, property, tourism and the Goan way of life. They had embraced the 'don't let the truth come in the way of a good story' anthem and 'if I repeat this often enough loudly and confidently, it will become true.' Our absolute faith in what we believe on social media, WhatsApp and Google as God's own truth only helps their cause. Goans also continue to be chauvinistic towards outsiders and those unlike them—almost xenophobic, they have become protectionists about Goa.

Over the last couple of years, there have been two contentious bills that have failed. Each tried to define Goans and their rights in Goa today. The Goa Revolutionary Party tried to introduce the Person of Goan Origin Bill (POGO19) to 'protect the rights of Goans'. Their manifesto was 'the

Goan is losing out to outsiders, not only in terms of culture but government jobs, comunidade lands, housing projects and schemes. Our identity, culture and tradition are fast fading.' They stated that a 'person of Goan origin of the State of Goa shall be a person whose parents or grandparents or either one of the parents or grandparents was born in Goa before 20 December 1961, or who had a permanent habitation in Goa before 20 December 1961, and is also a citizen of India'.*

The other bill, the Bhoomiputra Adhikari Bill in 2021 proposed granting housing to certain groups. It wanted to recognize anyone living in Goa for thirty years or more as a *bhoomiputra* (son of the soil) and give them the right to own their own 'dwelling unit'.† This proposed bill met with severe backlash and was withdrawn.

The premise of both these bills gives insight into the rising sentiments and politics of Goans in Goa today.

I know migration makes us multidimensional and builds a tolerant world. I was caught in the middle, defending Goans to everyone else and defending outsiders to Goans. Covid pushed us into a world of fear of everyone and everything different. It made us regard every new person with suspicion and think, 'Are we going to get the deadly virus from them?' As a society, we already live in silos. Social media is pushing us to become even more insular. We divide our world by

---

* 'Everything You Wanted To Know About Person of Goan Origin Bill 2019', Goa Prism, 24 June 2019, https://www.goaprism.com/everything-you-wanted-to-know-about-person-of-goan-origin-bill-2019/.
† 'The Goa Bhumiputra Adhikarini Bill, 2021', Legislative Assembly of the State of Goa, July 2021, https://www.goavidhansabha.gov.in/uploads/bills/1281_final_BN49OF2021-AP.pdf.

language, colour, education, occupation, neighbourhood and anything else we can find. The right-wing fear sweeping across the country and the world, breaking us by religion and race is real and it's chilling.

Original and newcomers, insiders and outsiders, us and them, old and new . . .

So many labels, so many divisions . . .

History is convenient. We never learn about entire communities and civilizations if they rely on storytelling and oral history and/or we do not know the language and/or their story if it does not fit the colonizer, historian, researcher, filmmaker or journalist's agenda. It is someone's version of the truth, their interpretation of what may or may not have happened. In our country and across the world, history seems to be written and rewritten every day from a political point of view. Over the last few years, I have reflected more closely on my conscious and unconscious biases. I started thinking about how stereotypes affect our perception of people and places, and how prejudice can lead to discrimination.

This is my herstory of living in Siolim today with my socio-economic, geopolitical, gender, race, religion and language biases. I realized that there were fallacies that popular culture and marketing brochures were perpetuating about Goa on the one hand, and the current political climate was trying to eliminate, on the other. The propaganda goes beyond the real world—it reaches us even in the Metaverse, where, with so many realistic deep fakes, I can't tell what's real and what's not. I don't know who an avatar or a hologram is, and which dimension we are communicating in. It is getting harder to know the truth. We are constantly scrolling, tapping and not listening to each other, while the artificial intelligence (AI) on our many devices is. Bots and apps are telling us what to eat, drink and wear, and how many steps we must walk. While Goan aunties and uncles are always outspoken and tell you what to do and not to do, they are now being outdone by the AI.

What's So Special about Goa, Anyway?

A good friend gushes, 'As soon as I land, I feel relaxed.' Another friend, Arun, smiles sheepishly and confesses, 'We bar crawled through those dives in Anjuna or was it Vagator? I don't remember the details but what a fun night!'

Goa = Beach + Party + Drink. Capital of hedonistic heaven. Ibiza of the East.

When friends visit, they assume I am always ready to party, beach and restaurant hop with them and that I can meet them anywhere at any time. The fact that Goa is a state, not a city, is lost. When I say, 'I am so sorry, but I have to juggle work with managing my house, garden and dogs. I can't make it to see you in the South. It's too far.' The repartee is always, 'What work in Goa? You are just making excuses. Acting pricey. Come ya, we are hanging in this cool shack in the day and then going drinking and dancing in the night. It's going to be so much fun.'

Every time I mention Goa, people's eyes light up and they break into a smile. Everyone I meet wants to tell me their own Goa story. Friends have waxed, 'Goa is a state of mind. A place like no other on the planet. A piece of paradise. There is music in the air.'

To understand how we got here, I will briefly outline the history and geography to set the stage and give a cultural, social and political context.

A Few History Highlights

With what little archaeological, literary and folklore evidence that exists—it all points to the Gauda, Kunbi, Velip and Dhangar tribes, collectively called the Kunbis, being the first settlers. They designed the Khazan technology for farming in Goa that we marvel at today. Khazans are coastal wetlands that have been reclaimed by an intricate system of dykes (*bandhs*), sluice gates (*manos*) and canals, and put to multiple productive uses such as agriculture, aquaculture and salt panning. The tides flowing in and out were able to support the original Khazans (saltwater paddy growing), the wetlands and mangroves.

Joseph Fernandes, who has devoted twenty-three years of his life thinking about the bandhs, explains, 'In 4000 BCE, when man was changing from hunter–gatherer to farmer, nature provided conditions for the settlers from the island of Divar to create rice fields from the large deposit of silt that settled in and around their island in front of Old Goa.'

Joe, who lives on the island of Chorão, continues, 'The legend suggests that a man came from the East on a white horse and brought this technique to Divar. He was then worshipped as a God and elevated to a *ganvdevāta**

---

* Village god.

as this invention saved farmers from toiling as the tides did the work. One must remember that the work of the bandhs took at least 1000 years. This was before they had the wheel, between 4000 and 2500 BCE.'*

The Gaudas and Kunbis have a distinct lifestyle as well as foods, clothes and jewellery. In recent years, there have been chefs and food tours that are trying to revive and showcase their food. Kunbi sarees, which were worn by the women of the Gauda community, have had an academic and haute couture revival today. Many urban middle-class women, including me, now choose to wear them. Unfortunately, this Kunbi saree resurgence does not benefit this original indigenous community, as they are now made across the border in Karnataka.

In Goa, there is an early history of cooperative lands owned by the original village dwellers labelled comunidade by the Portuguese. This land (*gaunkaris*) was collectively owned but controlled by the male descendants of those who claimed to be the founders of the village (predominantly from upper castes).

Villages were self-sufficient collective economic units. Members of the gaunkaris were called *gaunkars* or *zonnkars* and were entitled to a dividend (*zonn*). The system applied equally to agricultural land and village housing. In many villages, the share of the profits from these ancient cooperative fields continues to be paid annually but only to the males of that community. In those days, the cultivation of rice required a stable central authority, which was a position

---

* 'Khazan Lands', ActforGoa, https://actforgoa.org/resource/khazan-lands/, last accessed 12 September 2023.

claimed by these landowners. The monsoon months were crucial for planting as they provided water for the paddy, the main crop of the year.

I was fascinated to read in Celsa Pinto's *The Concise History of Goa* that these early settlers also believed in sacred groves, a part of the forest that was dedicated to the gods. We still have sacred groves in Goa and my prayer is that they remain sacred.

Similar to most ancient civilizations, early settlers lived off this fertile land and had animistic beliefs— they worshipped spirits to save them from the fury of the elements and had guardian spirits that they believed protected them. This mysticism of protector spirits persists in contemporary Goa. As organized religions conquered and imposed rituals, the culture absorbed these contradictory codes. Goa remains multidimensional and multicultural, a culmination of centuries of invasions and influences. Today, as we collectively worship the newest god of capitalism, our identity continues to be syncretic and our celebrations and festivals have roots in worshipping and blessing the land.

Archaeological and historical sources suggest that ports and trade centres existed along the estuaries and tributaries of the rivers. These ancient ports played a significant role in maritime trade. Early Hindu legends call the city of Goa, Gove, Govapuri and Gomantak while medieval Arabian geographers knew it as Sindabur or Sandābūr, and the Portuguese named it Velha Goa.

Ruled by the Kadamba dynasty from the second century CE to 1312 and then by Muslim invaders of the Deccan from 1312 to 1367, Goa was annexed by the neighbouring Hindu Vijayanagar empire and later conquered by the

Bahami sultanate, which founded Old Goa on the island in 1440.

After 1482, when the Bahami sultanate was divided, Goa became a part of the Muslim king, Adil Shah's kingdom of Bijapur. In March 1510, Old Goa was attacked by the Portuguese General, Afonso de Albuquerque,* after which their rule extended beyond Old Goa for over 400 years. Old Goa then became the capital of the Portuguese empire in Asia and citizens were granted the same civic privileges as those living in Lisbon.

Over the centuries, the Portuguese had a profound influence on Goa's culture, governance, traditions and beliefs. Today, there continues the debate about the inquisition and how the Portuguese converted Hindus (typically upper caste) to Catholicism in return for favours—land, tax exemptions and power. Over the next four centuries, there were sporadic revolts and Goa was finally liberated in December 1961 and became a part of the recently independent former British colony, India. Initially, as a union territory along with the Portuguese enclaves Daman and Diu, which were part of the Estado da India, and in 1987, as a state. I remember the day, 30 May 1987, when I was a young professional looking for a job to start my career in advertising in Bombay with no premonition of what it would mean to me today. Goa continues to have a tenuous relationship with Portuguese vs British colonial influences and the Indian nationalist identity.

---

* 'Goa | History, India, Map, Population, & Facts', Encyclopedia Britannica, https://www.britannica.com/place/Goa/History, last accessed 16 October 2023.

The 1960s saw a significant campaign launched for Konkani to be the language of the newly independent Goa and a fight against being swallowed up by the neighbouring giant, Maharashtra. In the historic early 1967 opinion poll, Goa voted to remain independent in governance and language, and Jack Sequeira was hailed as its father. The slogans went something like this: '*Amkam naka bhaji puri, Aleluia. Amkam zai xitkoddi, Alleluia*'* and '*Naka amka shrikhand puri, amchi xitt kodij bari*'.† On 4 February 1987, Konkani finally became the official language and found its due place in Goan history and identity. In Goa, it is written in Roman and Devanagari scripts. Just south of the border, in the Kannada script, further south in Malayalam and also in the Arabic script. Goans are historically multilingual, communicating in Konkani, Marathi, Portuguese, Hindi and English.

Also in the late 1960s, two acts were introduced in Goa in line with India's ideology as a socialist republic towards a fair distribution of land—the Mundkar Act that gave *mundkars* (tenants) a right to their dwelling place and the Agricultural Tenancy Act that gave the fields of landlords to the tiller.

Goa's Unique Geography

Goa's enviable Konkan coastline runs 160 km from north to south. Fertile soil and dense forests attract a kaleidoscope of birds and animals while the red earth filled with iron ore attracts plunder. South Goa has four wildlife sanctuaries—

---

* Konkani for 'We don't want puri bhaji, Alleluia, we want rice and curry, Alleluia'.
† Konkani for 'We don't want shrikhand puri (a Maharashtrian delicacy), we are happy with our rice and curry'.

Mhadei, Bhagwan Mahavir, Netravalli and Cotigao. The Salim Ali bird sanctuary is on the island of Chorão.

The state is administratively divided into two districts: north and south Goa, and further into twelve talukas. There are nine major (eleven in total) rivers running across Goa and it is protected by the Western Ghats in the east.

The Mandovi River is majestic and it is Goa's source of great love and pride. It hosts the capital, Panjim. With so many rivers, backwaters, lakes and intricate irrigation systems, life revolves around water. Over the years, the bridging of rivers and damming of lakes are a sign of slow but steady progress. The bridges across the two arterial rivers—the Mandovi and the Zuari—were constructed in my lifetime. Friends still reminisce, 'I remember the days when we took ferries. There were no bridges. We would wait patiently and watch life on the river while the ferries crossed back and forth fetching fish, people, cars and scooters.'

My Version of the Goa Tourism Story

The first starred hotel opened on 2 December 1952 to host officials for the tenth exposition of the relics of St Francis Xavier, the Spanish Jesuit priest who is popularly known as Goencho Saib,* he is revered in Goa till today. His death anniversary on 3 December is marked with a public holiday in the state and the exposition of his body continues to draw the faithful to Goa. The next exposition of St Francis

---

* Konkani for 'Lord of Goa'.

Xavier's sacred relics is planned from November 2024 to January 2025.

Goa attracted waves of people from across the world looking for paradise—the 'hippies' of the 1970s drove their Volkswagen vans to and in Goa. It was a cool place that fitted their bohemian ideology—pristine beaches, laid-back attitude, simple, village living. They brought with them their music, drugs, parties and the stereotypical sex, drugs and rock 'n' roll lifestyle that lingers on. Cousin Cedric has a faraway look in his eyes as he says, 'Those good old days when the hippies were on the beaches, you never knew who you would hear jamming. It could be George Harrison [from the Beatles]. I bought my first pair of Levi's at the Anjuna flea market.' Neil, a guy I ran into at Heathrow while we waited to board a flight recounted, 'I drove to Goa from London in the 1970s, across now inaccessible countries like Iran and Afghanistan. I try to come back every year. I rent in Siolim not far from you.'

I remember when, in the mid-1970s, the Taj group of hotels' five-star property—The Fort Aguada Beach Resort opened. Soon after in the early 1980s, Cidade de Goa came to Dona Paula and the Oberoi opened in Bogmalo. The Goa Tourism Development Corporation (GTDC) was set up in 1982. The 1983 Commonwealth Heads of State conference and Pope John Paul II's visit to Goa in 1986 put Goa on the European tourist map and tourism slowly became a primary source of income for many Goans.

Around the mid-1970s, shacks started springing up on the beaches as Goa didn't have restaurants for tourists to eat at and they have been gaining popularity since. An old school friend, Sangita, creates her perfect Goa vacation: 'All we want to do in Goa is go to the shacks, lie on those beach loungers, drink chilled Kingfisher, get massages and relax.' The shack licensing every year is a complicated, political auction. Today, they are an ecological hazard, causing beach erosion, noise and plastic pollution. Since most of these shacks violate the CRZ* coastal and environmental laws, the pollution board is pushing to demolish many.

The 1970s Bollywood blockbusters Raj Kapoor's *Bobby* and Manmohan Desai's *Amar, Akbar, Anthony* reinforced the Goan Catholic stereotype. *Dil Chahta Hai*, in the early 2000s, which followed three young Bollywood heartthrobs on a road trip to find themselves and love on the gorgeous beaches of Goa, further cemented the party cliché. The more recent Shahrukh Khan–Alia Bhatt movie, *Dear Zindagi,* has brought a rash of self-indulgent Instagrammers, YouTubers and tourists with selfie sticks to that *Maddani*† in Parra. Bollywood stereotypes made me wonder who Goans are and who I am—they had a cross-wearing, drunk villain, a short-skirted English-speaking secretary and a stoned, guitar-playing junkie. I did not identify with any of these stereotypes but that's how many perceived me.

From the late 1980s, Goa turned into a hub for charter flights for European tourists looking for low-budget, all-inclusive packages. Sue, who visits often, says, 'We love Goa. So cheap. We come by those Condor charters every year for the warm beaches and cold beers.' These transactions are

---

* Coastal Regulation Zone.
† Konkani for a road lined with coconut trees.

done in Europe, so they do not contribute significantly to the Goan economy.

The 1990s brought fresh waves of tourists and beach colonizers—Israelis, looking at tourism and music; others at the seamier side of drugs and arms. Goa Trance was a popular form of music for the party scene, with psychedelic lights to go with the psychedelic drugs.

Russians have been colonizing North Goa since the late 1990s with the first charter flight landing in 2001. Today, there are signs in Russian and some restaurants that allow only Russians to enter. They are the owners, staff and guests. Over the years, we have not been allowed entry into a couple of places near Morjim and Ashwem. When the war started in Ukraine in February 2022, memes were circulated on social media platforms with jokes about the Russian army waiting for reinforcements from Morjim, since Goa has been a refuge for Russians over the last twenty years. Now since the 2022 war, both Russian and Ukrainian refugees are permanently relocating to Goa.

Neighbourly gossip and newspapers allege that Sudanese and Nigerians are dabbling in drugs and arms alongside Russians.* The combination of loud tourists, nasty casinos, drugs and seamy nightlife in the North have paled the charm

---

* Sandeep Unnithan, 'Ruthless and Organised, Nigerians Have Become the Biggest Players in India's Market for Hard Narcotics', *India Today*, 30 November 2013, https://www.indiatoday.in/magazine/special-report/story/20131202-nigerians-drugs-narcotics-goa-police-drug-trafficking-nigerian-murder-768812-1999-11-29;
'Nigerian Held with Narcotics Worth Rs 66 Lakh', *Times of India*, 24 June 2023, https://timesofindia.indiatimes.com/city/goa/nigerian-held-with-narcotics-worth-rs-66-lakh/articleshow/101230421.cms?from=mdr#.

of calm Goan villages and beaches. The question is often asked: 'Is Goa moving from party city to Sin City a la Vegas with the casinos?'

In order to stop mining practices in Goa, the Goa Foundation went to the Supreme Court in September 2012. While the chief minister temporarily stopped mining that month, the Supreme Court ruled in October that the mining could not resume without its permission. The Goa Foundation won the case in April 2014 and when the mining was briefly restarted in 2015, it was shut down again by the Supreme Court in March 2018. With the major source of funds for the government dried up, the casinos became the new mines. The unplanned, unsustainable growth of construction and casinos accelerated the beginning of the end of the peaceful, pretty Goa.

Planes, cars and busloads of tourists descend on Goa every year just to gamble at the casinos. In March 2010, a *New York Times* '36 hours in Goa' piece featured one of Panjim's floating casinos.* I was living in London at the time and received emails from friends asking for my insider intel on the journalist's suggestions. In my response, I told them how the Goan in me was livid that the *NYT* recommended gambling as part of the Goa tourist agenda.

Today, we have every Indian and international hotel chain with multiple properties across Goa—from boutiques with a few rooms to conventions with hundreds of rooms. After the pandemic, Goa has further expanded its appeal and become an enticing conference and destination wedding

---

* Jeff Koyen, '36 Hours in Goa, India', *New York Times*, 11 March 2010, https://www.nytimes.com/2010/03/14/travel/14hours.html.

venue. In the season, every week friends drop in to visit when they are here for a conference, a reunion or a wedding.

More recently, Covid-19 has brought the rest of India to live in Goa. The young and old, nouveau riche and intellectual, artist and entrepreneur—they all came to Goa for its natural beauty, tolerance and cultural milieu and found a home. I came too and I am digging deeper to put down roots.

What's So Special about Goans Anyway?

'Nothing is simpler than being a Goan . . . For God, in his infinite sagacity, has divided the world into two continents, Goa and the rest of the world, and the whole of humanity into two distinct races: Goans and non-Goans,' writes poet and writer ManohaRai SarDessai in his guest column 'On being a Goan' in the *Goa Today*. He continues, 'A Goan, thinks a Goan, is the most perfect specimen in the human race . . . He alone is well mannered, intelligent, conversant with what is going on in the world and he alone *knows,* he alone knows how to enjoy life, he alone has the best of the two worlds, the East and the West.'[*]

A Goan's love for the state is our foremost attachment. Its breathtaking beauty has made us fiercely proprietorial. You will hear: 'Our Goa or our Goan.' Being Goan comes

---

[*] ManohaRai SarDessai, 'On being a Goan', *Goa Today*, May 1984. Goa Today was a hallmark monthly magazine founded by Lambert Mascarenhas and F. D. Dantas in 1966.

first, before our Hindu, Muslim, Christian, Sikh, Parsi, Jain, Jewish, Buddhist, atheist, or environmentalist beliefs. We are united by our love of this blessed land, its mangoes and feni. Goan men across religious and other persuasions have gout—the gift of a rich diet.

Goa is some sort of strange east–west hybrid, where Goans choose to define themselves as different people linguistically and culturally. Estranged from the rest of India because of its longer Portuguese colonization, Goan Catholics assimilated through social norms and adapted to Westernized dress and food habits after converting. Over the centuries, there was a synthesis with the Latin culture and Goa got the 'eat, drink, sing, dance and be merry' stereotype that we still have today. With its wine, women and songs, Goa is seen as more Western than the rest of India and is the exotic East for those from the West.

Goans have a unique sense of who we are. We have strong joie de vivre. To some, it is heritage—the land, *tambdi mati*,* Konkani, *mandos* and *dulpods*,† *kunbi* and *dekni*,‡ house and property, laterite, Xittcodi,§ feni, football and the monsoons. To others, it is modernity—education and transportation for all, accountable politics, the fight

---

* Konkani for red earth.
† Two types of Konkani music that also have dances. The mando is a musical form that evolved during the nineteenth and twentieth centuries among the Goan Catholics. It blends traditional Goan folk music with western musical traditions. The men wear formal coats and use a handkerchief as a prop, women wear Western dresses and use a fan. Instruments that accompany the mando are guitars, violins and the ghumot.
‡ Types of local dances.
§ Konkani for rice and curry.

against mining, construction, corruption and casinos. Many are proud: 'We have one of the highest rates of literacy, voter turnout and GDP in the country.'

The Goa Migration Study 2008 discusses,

> Though the Portuguese spent 451 years in Goa—making it one of the longest colonial dominations in history—the regime unleashed its proselytizing zeal only on its 'Old Conquests' in the talukas of Bardez, Salcete, Tiswadi and Mormugao. The Old Conquests were densely populated, but the Portuguese did little to set up industries or generate employment in these areas. Consequently, nearly one-tenth of the population was forced to migrate.*

This long history of the heartbreaks of Goans leaving Goa is captured in a very emotional Konkani mando. Every time I hear Goans sing 'Adeus Korchea Vellar' (The Time to Say Goodbye), they choke up. It expresses the anguish of a people who have known the price of separation from a land that is so beautiful and peaceful but lacks employment.

Goans migrated for economic reasons to find jobs. The biggest and most influential clusters went to where they could find education and/or employment—the sophisticated Bombay Goans (Bombaikars) with big city conveniences and attitudes, the Karachi Goans, who now have Indian visa and passport-related challenges and complications with their land being confiscated and labelled 'enemy property', and the East African Goans (Africanders), who are Westernized

---

* K. Mohandas, 'Goa Migration Study: 2008', Department of NRI Affairs, Panaji, Government of Goa, 2009.

in their dress and attitude. Many Africanders prefer to be called Goans and not Indians. Then there were also Goans like my grandparents who moved to Poona, Belgaum, or Nagpur for education and employment.

Academicians and historians have studied and documented the Goan diaspora, including prominent personalities of Goan descent. While many hold public office, including the re-elected Prime Minister of Portugal, Antonio Costa, several others are soldiers, artists, writers, musicians, athletes, doctors, engineers, nuns and priests, who have made the world a better place, saved lives and won hearts and accolades. Uncle Clarie, my godfather, Mummy's younger brother aka Wing Commander Clarence D'Lima, was an elite and decorated Indian airforce pilot, who laid down his life (at the young age of thirty-nine) in the service of this country. In November 1977, he was piloting an aircraft carrying then-prime minister Morarji Desai and other VVIPS that crashed close to the storm-soaked Jorhat airfield in Assam, as they attempted to land under extremely adverse and challenging flight conditions. All the passengers survived while all the flight crew perished. In honour of his heroic service, a road is named after him in Pune (close to where he lived) and in Limavaddo in Porvorim, Socorro, Goa (his ancestral village).

Plenty of the Goan diaspora remain very interested in their ancestry. Committed to the cause, they spend time, effort and money building a family tree that goes back generations and centuries, digging through church, public and family records, and photographs. They research their family history to the time before their ancestors were converted to Catholicism and find their Hindu last names.

Nowadays, they even use technology, online family trees and DNA testing to prove how Goan they are. They organize family reunions in Goa, Portugal or both. Louis, a friend from Bengaluru, says, 'Some 100 of us long lost cousins from across the world all met for three days after Christmas. We took over the whole resort in Benaulim. So many of us had never met before.' The more the merrier is the motto here. Others don't speak to their siblings, squabbling over ancestral property or carrying generational grudges. A cousin is heartbroken as he says, 'I don't even know why my uncle [dad's brother] and his wife don't talk to us, and no one seems to remember why. They are all in their eighties now and he has cancer but still refuses to talk. I have tried to reach out, but they won't even let me enter their house.'

As Goans look back with saudade, academic papers, books* and films document their different lifestyles and their connection to their Goan identity. Prominent landowner families,† typically the elite in Panjim and Salcette, have been quoted saying that they preferred 'the good old Portuguese days', when they had special privileges and lavish lifestyles during colonial times. They preferred to be Portuguese and not Indian.

For many of the diaspora, being Goan is their strongest identity—it ranks above being Aussie, Brit, Kiwi or Canuck. Taking with them the food, language, music, customs and traditions, they create a little Goa in their unfamiliar lives

---

* Stella Mascarenhas-Keyes, *Colonialism, Migration & the International Catholic Goan Community* (Goa: Goa, 1556, 2011).
† William Dalrymple, 'At Donna Georgina's, Fort Aguada, Goa, 1993', *The Age of Kali: Indian Travel and Encounters* (New Delhi: Penguin Books India, 2004).

and homes. There are Goan associations that celebrate village feasts with dances and picnics, sorpotel, vindaloo and good music. They are torn between accepting their new world and hanging on to the old, wondering if they belong in either or neither. There are some who want to have nothing to do with Goa. They want no part of the laid-back stereotype and intrusive culture. They insist, 'We don't even want to visit. Such a backward place. There is a whole world to travel to, so why would we come to Goa? Coming there is so awkward—excruciating family visits, nosy questions and other dreadful obligations.'

As an anglicized expat Goan, before I moved here during the pandemic, I had had superficial experiences, as do many, since our parents, grandparents or great-grandparents left Goa. Goa was a place you went on holiday or to take care of responsibilities. It was not a place you lived in. Our Goan experiences were based on the occasional or annual holiday, which included visiting relatives, reminiscing, eating Goan food and going to the beach. Others we knew also came to Goa to arrange marriages and visit graveyards. However, as soon as two Goans meet, no matter where on the planet, the first question is: 'Which village are you from?' This is quickly followed by 'Which vaddo?'* These innocuous questions decide your place on the socio-economic-class-caste table.

Once they know your village and vaddo, the follow-up question is, 'Do you know Dr Mascarenhas [or Fernandes, Dias, Noronha]? He is my wife's mother's brother-in-law's cousin's neighbour.' All Goans seem to be related

---

* Konkani for a ward, a smaller administrative division in a village in Goa or a modern-day neighbourhood.

or connected—either through marriage, ancestry, village
or vaddo. We look for connections and cousins wherever
we go as it brings a strong sense of belonging. Everyone
knows everyone. You can run, but you can't hide from your
Goa-ness.

Lore suggests that the Goan Catholics converted on
condition that they could continue with the caste system. It
helped the upper castes to keep their power and privileges.
During marriage proposals, it often rears its ugly head. This
archaic system has also spread to the diaspora. I unwittingly
witnessed a nosy matchmaking acquaintance in Pune
whispering, 'We only want a boy from a good family like
ours; you know what we mean.' I thought to myself, 'I don't
know, nor do I want to know.' I'm always sad that a chance
of birth is used as another way to judge and discriminate.
But it exists in 2023.

Poet and teacher Eunice de Souza used her art to call out
both the patriarchy and these prejudices.

Here are the first eleven lines from her popular poem
'Marriages are Made', which is taught in college curricula:*

My cousin Elena
is to be married
The formalities
have been completed:
Her family history examined
for T.B. and madness

---

* Eunice de Souza, 'Marriages are Made', Government Degree College
Kulgam, http://gdckulgam.edu.in/Files/f07ef270-7e91-4716-8825-
2966f17cc0f7/Custom/Eunice%20de%20Souza%20(Marriages%20
are%20Made).pdf.

her father declared solvent
her eyes examined for squints
her teeth for cavities
her stools for the possible
non-Brahmin worm.

Despite our complicated class, caste and migration hierarchies, Goans are sentimental about their roots. They long for *amchem goem*,* call themselves OCGs—Overseas Citizens of Goa—and believe that Goa is the centre of the universe.

Defining Goans Through Labels, Stereotypes and Symbols

Pop culture stereotypes have created a myth that Goa is predominantly Catholic while in reality, Hinduism has always been the dominant religion. There is also a strong Muslim presence. Though we may all worship in different ways, we live almost the same lives, eat the same fish, speak the same language and live in harmony with each other and the land we all love.

I was recently reassured of how closely the two major religions coexist, when I read the distinguished Konkani writer, Damodar Mauzo's translated short stories in English. Living and running a grocery store in Majorda, a largely Catholic village, he writes with profound insight into the Catholic community and eloquently fictionalizes the real and existential issues they grapple with. This amazing writer

---

* Konkani for 'our Goa'.

and human was awarded the prestigious Jnanpith Award in 2022* and continues to write and speak fearlessly against the divisive politics in Goa.

Looking at other popular Goan stereotypes, a contentious one is susegad. Goans resent it as it labels us laid-back and not ambitious. A friend pleads, 'Please don't call us susegad, we are always portrayed as lazy.' On a positive note, being content, peaceful, relaxed and chilled is something we should all aspire to in today's anxious, hyperconnected world. If it leads to a state of well-being, it is an attitude worth adopting.

The final straw for any self-respecting Goan is the sheer horror of being called Goanese. Somehow, to be called Goanese is a serious insult. While some say it is a combination of Goan and Portuguese, as a term it is hugely resented.

I read that the Portuguese brought their pao to Goa originally to the Catholics in Salcette. The Jesuits taught baking to families in Majorda as they missed their crusty bread and needed someone to make it for them and to distribute as hosts for Holy Communion during mass. They could not get the yeast needed to make the bread rise so they used local fermented toddy—bringing the pao its special Goan flavour. With the rising cost and decreasing availability of good toddy today, this heritage is declining and ironically, yeast is now used to bake bread across Goa. Pao is still handmade and baked in a wood-fired stone oven.

Poi is perceived to be healthier since it's made with wholemeal rather than white flour. Our humble poi has

---

* The highest literary award in India.

The poder on his evening bread rounds

become symbolic and over-popular in a post-pandemic Goa. Breakfast Instagram posts make Goans blanche, 'What is this fancy avo-poi, now?' and 'They don't even know how to pronounce poi, it is po-eee. They say, poy (as in joy) or pohi, where is the h sound coming from?'

Diasporic Goans have their own stereotype to grapple with. Pao is a popular label for Goans in Mumbai because they originally owned bakeries and ate pao. Other labels include macapao (mac for short) and paowalla. They all started by being derogatory and discriminatory but now we are taking control and owning them.

In Goa, the poder with his basket of fresh pao blowing the horn (the sound of the horn is a loud pow pow and very typical) and cycling around every morning and evening, is a significant component of culture and identity. His basket also carries *katre* (bread cut with a pair of scissors), *undo* (crusty bread) and *kankon* (bread that looks like a bangle or a bagel, very hard).

The different types of pao available in Goa

You will find a symbolic garrafão,* bharni[†] (that has evolved to either a vase or some sort of objet d'art) and azulejo[‡] as a house sign in every fancy hotel, shop, home or salon. Often, I see old-style traditional round grinding stones[§] (*rogddo*) as garden adornments and wonder if

---

* Portuguese for a large jug, bottle or jar.
† Konkani word for jar.
‡ Portuguese for a typical, blue-painted tile.
§ Large stone mortar and pestles traditionally used to grind masalas together.

this is tokenism to the local culture or integration to the adopted one.

Village Goans are today baffled when they hear terms like organic or homegrown. 'We have been growing these coconuts, chikoos, ponnos* and custard apples on our trees for years. Tending them with love and our own natural manure. Our hens run free. They give us eggs, and we eat and sell extra. Why are people asking now if we are selling organic and free range? Nowadays, I even hear people saying cage-free. Why are they eating jackfruit raw? What is this vegan meat? We only eat jackfruit ripe as a fruit.' They go on, 'We make our own coconut oil by drying the coconuts we get from our trees. Now they ask for extra virgin, cold-pressed coconut oil. How is it different and why is it better than the one we make?'

Fishing is an immensely popular Goan hobby. In Siolim, in the early mornings and late evenings, you see boys and men sitting with their fishing rods, waiting patiently over the creek, backwaters and river. My neighbours are excited about their weekend fishing trips and often invite me along.

Bharat loves cycling. You know the saying, 'You can take the boy out of Pune, but you can't take out Pune from the boy.' In September 2020, when he went to Decathlon, he realized that beyond the sourdough starter and toilet paper crisis, Covid-19 had also created a cycle crisis. Not to be deterred by this, he ordered it online and when the cycle arrived, he started exploring Siolim and the neighbouring villages. These days, he enjoys having chai and chatting at

---

* Konkani for jackfruit.

Cycling down our road

small cafes and village stalls in the mornings, while taking in the view and catching up on local gossip.

We have also discovered the many shortcuts and by-lanes off the main busy roads while walking our lab Haruki every day. Now that we are resident Goans, people smile and wave at us as we walk or cycle past them while they are busy sweeping the leaves in their gardens. We naively chose to have white compound walls, which quickly turned greenish-grey. I always wondered how my neighbours' white walls remained pristine till I saw them whitewashing them every year—our Hindu neighbours before Ganesh

Chaturthi and Diwali, and the Catholics before Christmas. They also regularly paint the white crosses and colourful Tulsi *vrindavans** in front of their homes so they remain fresh.

Finding Symbols

In any shop, bank or government office, it is easy to spot the Goan women who all wear their gold jewellery as a symbol of their identity. While Hindu women wear a *mangalsutra*, typically with a little coral and/or pearl, Catholic women wear a gold chain with a cross around their necks. Both will have gold earrings, bangles and rings on. As I have embraced my Goan roots, I have spent too much time and money at the fantastic De Jewel in Miramar, recommended to me by my Pune school bestie, Radha. There, I have restrung, reset, polished and fixed clasps and missing stones for some of Mummy's heirloom jewellery that Ingrid and I inherited. When I wear them to weddings, I am often envied, 'Wow, look at those corals and that *fator* (malachite), just gorgeous.' Aai often spoke with reverence about Goan jewellers—their craftsmanship and skill are legendary. The Portuguese took them to Portugal, where they created detailed designs with their fine workmanship.

As you saunter through Siolim, you observe the many imposing lions on gateposts of old Goan houses. Some also have roosters or saluting soldiers. Most of them are made of

---

* The tulsi is considered to be a sacred plant with rich mythological and religious associations. A tulsi is usually planted at the entrance of a Hindu Goan house in specially made colourful planters known as tulsi vrindavans.

The lion sentinels guarding Goan houses

terracotta and stone and are painted. A sign of majesty and opulence as well as a symbol of the Kadamba era, the lions seem to be guarding the house. The rooster or the cockerel, the national bird of Portugal was supposedly a popular addition to the Catholic houses during the Portuguese era while the soldado* played the protector as soldiers symbolize protection. You may also spot dogs, gargolyes, birds and angels on gateposts. Our house never had any of

---

* Portuguese for a soldier.

these sentinels—probably too humble to need protection. We see some new, fierce, huge lions being installed on modern gateposts that are truly opulent. Lions seem to be the most popular in Siolim and neighbouring Assagao. If someone says, 'Do drop in. Ours is the house with the lions on the gates', be very careful and ask for more details. I once got lost looking for the lions on the main Assagao road as I drove past houses previously owned by relatives and old friends from Pune, as I never realized so many of them had lions on their gateposts.

Happens Only in Goa

Living in Goa, you also need to understand and appreciate the concept of *falea*—which is Konkani for tomorrow, but is interpreted as 'why do today, what you can do tomorrow'. It takes some getting used to but helps to calm down all that urban angst we all seem to have.

Many Goans believe punctuality is elastic—two opposites somehow coexist. While some are fiendish to not live out the Goan susegad stereotype and get to you bang on time, others have embraced the tag and arrive up to three hours after a social or official appointment. No apology. Just a look of 'Relax. This is Goa only'. You need to be prepared for both. Go with the flow.

I have spent extended amounts of time over the last twenty years in Siolim before moving here full-time. Over this period, I have made some anecdotal observations and have manufactured my own criteria for being Goan. I need to emphasize that these are all tongue-in-cheek observations. While there is much research on Goans, our

My three dogs Roo, Rusty and Haruki

history, migration and diaspora, I rely on none of them. Also, here I am talking about Goans in their true salt of the earth, 'children of the soil' avatar living in the village, not the global diaspora who may identify as Goans in spirit but may have never lived here, or the more sophisticated Goans living in cities.

I fulfil some of these criteria but aspire to all:

- You speak Konkani.
- You notice car number plates and are suspicious of every car that does not have a GA (Goa) registration.
- You have at least two dogs and/or two cats. You may also have some pigs, hens, goats and cows.
- You eat fish, at least five days a week if not seven, and know what is seasonal and how it needs to be cooked— fried or curried. You know what fish is available in the market that day, how much it costs and how fresh it is just by looking at the gills.

- You know when all the religious festivals take place and how they are to be celebrated—the prayers, the customs and what to cook. There are a few every month—all celebrated with great pomp and pageantry—food, music and flowers.

- You can recognize not just the fruit but also the leaves of the mango trees in your neighbourhood. You know not only your own trees but also your neighbour's trees, who have the best Mancurad, Manghilar, Maldez, Bishop or Fernandinho. You track the flowers every year. You covet your neighbour's Mancurad tree, even breaking a commandment. You know which mangoes are to be just cut and eaten, and which ones you need to make the popular korum,* miskut,† or mangaad.‡ This also extends to other tropical fruit and berry trees— jackfruit, jamun, bimli, tamarind and carvanda.

- You have an encyclopaedic knowledge of all local flora and fauna and can identify birds and their sounds.

- You know exactly when the urak/feni supply starts each year and you have the best source. You drive for hours to get it but it's worth it. You brag about your source but don't share the contact as it's a closely guarded secret. You insist that only yours is genuine, 'the real stuff'.

- You sing with great gusto—in the shower, in church, at all celebrations, in a choir or a band. You play at least one musical instrument, usually a piano, guitar, violin or drums, and love music.

---

* Chopped-up raw mango in brine.
† Konkani for mango pickle.
‡ Konkani for mango jam.

- You have love/hate relationships with your neighbours and your family. You are either not talking to them and/or you know too much about them, or both. 'Keep your friends close and your enemies closer' is the mantra you follow.

- You know all your living and dead relatives at least up to the last five generations; who married whom, who was supposed to marry whom, where they live, when and where someone died, where they are buried and so on. You also know these details, including any scandals and dirt about your neighbours and friends.

- You know how to make (or who in the village makes) the best coconut oil, sausages, vinegar, bebinca,* xacuti and samarache† masala. You know which gaddo‡ has the best street food—cutlet pao, choris pao, ros omelette§ and patal bhaji¶ breakfast in your village/state. You have no interest in any other food or cuisine and look dismissively as new restaurants and cuisines debut in Goa.

- You refer to the months of October to March as the 'season'. It was historically the time tourists descended on Goa.

---

* Bebinca is a Goan delicacy. It is a slow-baked cake with 7–16 layers made from a batter of flour, sugar, ghee, egg yolk and coconut milk, and flavoured with nutmeg. Traditionally made during Christmas, it is now available year-round due to its growing popularity.

† A distinctive flavour made from dry roasting up to twenty-one spices and usually made with dried prawns and coconut milk.

‡ Konkani for cart.

§ Goan street food.

¶ Goan breakfast.

- You have a good appetite for and very strong opinions on local politics that you are always willing to share. You get your news only from the local papers (usually *OHeraldo*) and news channels (often Prudent media).
- You attend more funerals than wedding masses and wear black for funerals. For Christmas and weddings, you pull out your polyester suits or shiny, synthetic, sequined, lacy dresses and gowns.
- Lorna belting out 'Bebdo'* is your favourite anthem. In fact, you love anything Lorna sings. You sing, laugh and cry out loud every time you watch *Nachom-ia-Kumpasar.*†
- You religiously follow and play football, and support Brazil in the World Cup.
- You have jet-black hair, no matter your age.
- You have a healthy distrust for all outsiders. An outsider is a generic term used in Goa that covers anyone who is not Goan by ancestry. It does not discriminate based on socio-economic status, how long you have lived here, if you speak Konkani, have the required legal government identification and documentation, or own property. It's somehow beyond that.

---

* Bebdo means 'drunkard' in Konkani. The song speaks about serious issues of drunk husbands but has a fun, lively tune. In Goa, artists portrayed serious societal issues in a lighter tone to make more people aware.
† Konkani for 'Let's dance to the rhythm'. It is a Konkani musical drama directed by Bardroy Barretto based on the lives of two jazz musicians, Chris Perry and Lorna Cordeiro during the height of the Goan music scene in Bombay in the 1960s–70s. The title is the name of one of their songs.

I have made a start to claiming my local Goan—Niz Goenkar* status. I now complain, as well as the next Goan, about the rapid overdevelopment, pollution, politics and corruption at every level across the state. And of course, about outsiders.

---

* Konkani for resident Goan or real Goan.

Finding Siolim Stories and Legends

On the road to labelling myself a Niz Goenkar and Shivolkar,* I realized that I knew embarrassingly little about Goa. Grappling with centuries of history, hearsay, folklore, customs and traditions of a multidimensional Goa was overwhelming, so I concentrated on my home ground—Siolim. Here are the pieces I put together for some village pride—some facts, some legends:

- It is strategically located in the northwest of Goa, on the south bank of the fish-laden Chapora.
- Famous for its feni from coconut plantations, wooded hills with their wonderful komorebi through the seasons, extensive paddy fields and therapeutic springs.
- Fishing, foraging for shellfish, toddy tapping and distilling palm feni were the original occupations.
- A person from Siolim is known as a Siolcar, Shivalkar, Shivolkar or Xivolkar. With so many languages, scripts,

---

* Konkani for someone from Siolim.

cultures and influences, Siolim is also spelt as Shivolim and Xiolim.

- Local lore claims that Siolim got its name from the lions that lived in the hills here. They believe the word 'Siolim' is the combination of two words 'Xinv' and 'Halli'. In Konkani, Xinv (pronounced Shiu) means lion and Halli means place.* One argument that supports this hypothesis is that the village on the other side of the Siolim hill is called Vagali, which may be fusing Vag[†] and Halli.[‡] So, Tiger Village is over the hill from Lion Village. One tale goes that a wandering tiger fell into a well. It was found by a motley crew of drunken villagers. They gallantly claimed they had felled the beast. That's how there is a family of Vagmares (tiger hunters) over the hill. Oral history reports a tiger was spotted in the Marna thicket in 1902. The villagers panicked and plotted to get rid of the wild cat. A band of Siolkars hunted down the poor lost feline. In the past, lions and tigers used to roam the streets of Siolim. Even now, there are rumours of dogs disappearing, assumed to be eaten by hungry leopards. Sometimes a stray tiger is also allegedly spotted. I believe that some of the two-legged predators that I see around town are far more dangerous.
- Other legends suggest that Shivolim got its name from the Shiv-ling (the symbol of the mighty God Shiva).

---

* Konkani for village or place.
[†] Konkani for tiger.
[‡] 'Siolim', Wikipedia, 3 July 2023, https://en.wikipedia.org/wiki/Siolim.

- Today's Greater Siolim has grown to include three panchayats (Marna, Sodiem and Oxel) and parishes as well as nine vadde and two comunidades (Marna and Sodiem).
- It has a long history of churches, temples, convents, chapels, homes for the aged and schools.
- Holy Cross Convent established in 1933 was the pioneering school for girls' education in Goa. It included boarding, which attracted women from all over Goa and across borders. Today, it is coed. Other schools are St Francis Xavier (SFX), Vasant Vidyalaya, Keerti Vidyalaya and Shanta Vidyalaya.
- Siolim has several temples including the Shri Datta temple in Marna, the Satteri Devi temple in Gausovaddo, the Zagreshwar temple in Guddem, the Laxmi Narayan on the main road in Portavaddo, Ajoba temple right behind our house on the Sodiem Road and Shree Swami Samarth Math below the bridge to Chopdem.
- The bridge that joins Siolim to Chopdem over the Chapora, making it so easy to get to the beaches of the North, came as recently as 2002. After that, their popularity exploded. Over the last twenty years, they have gone the Baga way with throbbing Bollywood music, shops selling hats, bikinis, Hawaiian shirts and cargo shorts, and neon signs with flashing arrows pointing to a party or a bar.

Churches and Chapels

Standing tall and majestic, looking resplendent and regal, is the recently refurbished St Anthony's church. St Anthony is

The legend of Saint Anthony in Siolim

the patron saint of lost things and is famous for his thirteen miracles. Siolim church is the only one in the world where you will see a statue of St Anthony of Padua, the Portúguese-born Franciscan monk, holding a serpent on a rope in his hand. This miracle was acknowledged by the papal office where St Anthony and the snake have a special mention.

The version of this legend that I was told by my father and grandfather was that, when the church was being built, every morning the construction would be undone.

This traumatized the priests and workers as they wondered who was destroying their hard work overnight. In their desperation, they prayed to St Anthony and put a statue of him on-site, promising to dedicate the church to him. The next morning, when they returned to work, they found the statue of St Anthony with a snake on a rope in his hand (some versions allege it was a cobra). The construction proceeded to plan with the statue taking a place of prominence in the church. It also holds many visuals, statues and paintings commemorating this and many of Saint Anthony's miracles.

This quote from the church's website gives some background to my version:

> In 1600, the Franciscans (priests) planned to build a centrally located church for the Christians of Siolim but lacked sufficient funds. Coincidentally at the same time, two Portuguese merchants, sailing to Goa with a statue of St Anthony, were caught in a life-threatening storm in the Arabian Sea. They implored St Anthony, vowing to build a church in his honour at the closest point wherever they touched land if they survived the storm. They safely entered the river Chapora's Tributary, Fenduem. And in fulfilment of their vows, they contributed towards the construction of the church in honour of St Anthony. The church in Siolim was rebuilt after 300 years.*

My friend Brenda has great faith in St Anthony and says this prayer every time she loses something, 'Tony, Tony, turn

---

* 'St Anthony Church - Siolim - Mass Timings', ChurchTimings, 12 August 2019, https://www.churchtimings.com/st-anthony-church-siolim/.

around something's lost and it's got to be found.' He finds everything that is lost. Another friend, Rowena exclaims, 'Oh my God, in school, I can't tell you the number of times we prayed thirteen Hail Marys to St Anthony. Whatever it was that was lost, it was somehow found.'

His feast is celebrated with great fervour in Siolim and across the world on the Sunday following 13 June every year. In Siolim, there are trezenas—thirteen days of prayers leading up to the feast. Another cousin tells me 'Every Tuesday when I am in Goa I come to your church for mass.' Tuesday is St Anthony's Day.

All days of the year, the Catholic church celebrates the feast of a saint or a martyr and the faithful flock for mass to pray to that saint on their day. In today's times, there are WhatsApp posts with a picture and a prayer to that saint. Additionally, I am told: 'Litanies are prayed in homes to celebrate birthdays, anniversaries, recoveries, successes and there are vespers* in the evenings in the church to pray before the feasts.' You may understand why historically village life revolved around the church and still does for many.

Sunday mass obligation is a cornerstone for Catholics. No matter where you are travelling in the world, you need to find a church and go to mass on a Sunday. I have heard Sunday mass in Vietnamese, French and Spanish. In November 2021, the Siolim church started an English mass on Saturday evenings (to fulfil the Sunday mass obligation) and English masses for Christmas, Holy Week and Easter. At the same time, they also started a monthly mass in Hindi on Sundays and for all big feasts, so that the growing

---

* Konkani for evening prayers.

population of Hindi-speaking migrant labour had a place to worship and build fellowship. Our house help here, Ajit and Reshma, who are from Jharkhand, have found a community to celebrate their many feasts and observances in Goa. Early on 15 August 2022, Ajit put on his sneakers, packed a water bottle, got on a bus and headed for a football tournament. It was played in a large field outside of Margao. That night he came home with two kilos of mutton. He explained, '*Hum log Siolim se gaye* bus *banake*. Bus *mein hum 15–20 log the. Yaha Goa key alag alag gaon sey teams aaye they. Sab log Jharkhand, Chhattisgarh aur Orissa ke the. Vaha,* ladies *log, idli, vada ghar mein bana key bech rahe the. 100–200 log the 10–15 ek* team *mein. Jo* team *jeet gaya usko ek bakri ka* prize *mila* [We had all gone from Siolim, they had organized a bus to take us. There were around 15–20 of us on the bus. Over there, people had come from different villages across Goa. We were all from Jharkhand, Chhattisgarh and Orissa. There were some ladies who were selling homemade idlis and vadas. There were about 100–200 people in some 10–15 teams. Each team that won a game got a goat as a prize].' Ajit and I enjoyed mutton curry that day as his team had won their round. Reshma explained that this happens regularly in their village on 15 August, in the church compound, where girls and boys both play football on teams for the tournament and prizes include a goat.

Ajit and Reshma were also part of the community that celebrated the *Karam* aka *Karma* festival here in October 2022 and 2023. This is a harvest festival celebrated in Jharkhand, West Bengal, Madhya Pradesh, Chhattisgarh, Assam and Odisha for good harvest and health. The celebration includes going to the jungle accompanied by groups of drummers and cutting one or more branches of the Karam tree after worshipping it, which is recreated in the St Anthony's church. Reshma explains that the rituals include cutting a small part of a tree and bringing it back to the church to bless it. Then there are folk songs and dances around the symbols of this harvest festival (typically wood, fruit and flowers).

On a Saturday evening in November 2021, I went to the English mass in St Anthony's church. As a believer in Jesus Christ, I have faith that he welcomes all, saint and sinner alike. However, I was taken aback when I arrived at the church and saw a 4-foot-tall sign at the entrance that laid out a strict dress code and discouraged visitors and tourists. To make matters worse, a security guard enforcing the dress code deemed my dress too short and would not allow me to enter the church to attend the mass. After arguing that I was not a visitor or a tourist, I managed to get in.

For me, it is getting harder to have faith in a colonial, patriarchal institution that continues to be plagued by paedophilia and abuse, does not allow women to have reproductive choices nor is ready for women's authority, same-sex marriages or divorce. I wonder why I still go, though infrequently now. I realize it is because I find the mass calming, almost meditative. The physical church offers a peaceful, prayerful ambience. The rituals and familiar routines are comforting and reassuring in troubling times. The singing out loud of the hymns, standing, sitting, kneeling, reciting the 'Our Father' and responding with the Amens in unison in a congregation are all restorative. Even though I am sceptical about the institution, I am reassured by Pope Francis' commitment to preserving the environment and calling out European governments to accept refugees who are fleeing their countries because of persecution. He continues to urge world leaders to treat climate change as an emergency and reduce the use of fossil fuels. In October 2023, he was quoted as being open to blessing same-sex couples, but conservatives remain opposed.*

Another religious Siolim landmark on the hill (Dongormarg) is the Matteche Chapel, which is barely 500 metres behind our house. As a kid, I remember climbing up the hill with my parents. Years later, when I tried to find a way to hike up during a visit, I realized that the way I knew was overgrown with weeds and littered with garbage, making it impossible to find. Some years ago, my neighbour, Anthony Coelho, took me to the Stations of the Cross[†] on Ash Wednesday,[‡] held on the steps leading up to the chapel (there are now over 300 steps cut into the hill). I enjoyed the novel Stations of the Cross, the feeling of community, and the hymns and prayers in Konkani. The stations start at the foot of the hill. The last (fourteenth) station is at the top, followed by a mass in front of the chapel. You get a

---

* 'Pope Francis Suggests Gay Couples Could Be Blessed in Vatican Reversal', *Guardian*, 3 October 2023, https://www.theguardian.com/world/2023/oct/03/pope-francis-suggests-gay-couples-could-be-blessed-in-vatican-reversal.

† Stations of the Cross, also called Way of the Cross, is a devotional exercise of visiting and praying in front of each of the fourteen stations and meditating on the Passion of Christ. It stems from the practice of early Christian pilgrims who visited the scenes of the events in Jerusalem and walked the traditional route from the supposed location of Pilate's house to Calvary.

‡ Ash Wednesday is the first day of Lent, six and a half weeks before Easter. It is observed with ashes and fasting and is a reminder of one's own mortality.

panoramic view of Siolim and the Chapora, right up to Morjim and Camurlim. Haruki, one of my three dogs, loves this walk in the cooler weather. He skips to the top while I pant and puff on my way up.

Further down the road in Oxel, with a far-reaching view of the Chapora, the Arabian Sea and the valley, is the Our Lady of the Sea church. Right below is one of Siolim's therapeutic springs. 'We go regularly to dip in these medicinal waters,' says a long-time Siolkar, 'it keeps us healthy.'

Overlooking Siolim's illustrious Holy Cross convent is the Mae De Deus (Mother of God) chapel. On this plot, there is a cross with an inscription that commemorates the fact that the Franciscan priests built the first church in Siolim here in 1568.

The current-day Mae De Deus chapel, built in the same compound, observes two unique traditions. The first is that the Gausovaddo community gathers in front of the grotto of Our Lady of Fatima in front of the chapel in October every year and says the rosary. In other vaddos in Siolim and villages in Goa, the statue of Our Lady goes from house to house in October every year. The second is that on the first Sunday of May, a bride (the first girl from Gausovaddo to be married after this feast) wearing her white bridal gown, climbs up a ladder and places a crown of white roses on the statue of Our Lady of Fatima's head. This novel celebration was started in May 1944 and carries on till date.

Agricultural festivities are an important part of the church calendar as well. The blessing of the crop on 15 August as part of the Novachem Fest has origins in this agricultural history. My neighbours explain: 'The priest goes in a procession with a statue of St Anthony to bless the rice corn in the fields. There is also a brass band that plays for the occasion. The priest cuts a handful, and other parishioners cut some more and fill the basket. They go back to the church and distribute the blessed sheaves to the congregation.'

Famous Shivolkars

No village account is complete without a 'roll of honour', a list of 'eminent Goans', or 'prominent Goans'. These lists are historically predominantly male, hence I am always sceptical about them, but in the quest to become a good Goan, here goes my abridged list of eminent men in Siolim.

Siolim has famous musicians, ministers, footballers, teachers, doctors and bishops. Living legends include charismatic musician Remo, satirist Alexyz and the talented fashion designer Savio Jon. Other notable mentions are prominent journalist, *OHeraldo* editor Alister Miranda, well-known tiatrist* Kid Boxer (Caetano Manuel Pereira), the prestigious St. Xavier's College Bombay's librarian, popularly known as a walking encyclopaedia, Dominic Fernandes, as well as Siolim chronicler and St Anthony's church sacristan, Sebastian D'Cruz, who from 1982 to 2007 compiled ten souvenirs/books of his version of Siolim's parish and village history.

I was thrilled to know that Siolim's first woman doctor, Dr Elvira Dias, is alive and well. Her son, Dr Luis Dias, explains. 'My mother was the first female doctor from

---

* Tiatr is the most popular form of Konkani musicl theatre. A person who performs in a tiatr is called a tiatrist.

the village of Siolim. She was born in Nairobi, Kenya, in October 1932, but came to Siolim for her matriculation in the late 1940s. She topped her school, Holy Cross Convent Siolim, went to Wadia College in Pune, and later to Nair and Sion hospitals in Bombay to study medicine. Her plan was to come back to Siolim and practise as a GP from her *Godgoddo** House, close to her alma mater. But when she won a gold medal in Obstetrics and Gynaecology from Bombay University, she decided to specialize in it. From there, she went to Berlin (then West Berlin, West Germany) in 1962 and married my father, Dr Manuel Dias. Our family returned to Goa in 1970. She continued to practise and teach at Goa Medical College (GMC) until her retirement in 1990, after which she went into private practice in Panjim. Mama was still practising when Covid-19 hit in 2020. She turned ninety-one in October 2023.'

Siolkar writer, musician, playwright and lyricist, Reginaldo Fernandes, was a cultural giant in the world of Konkani music and literature. He was known as the 'Romansincho Patxai' (Emperor of Konkani novels). The road from Siolim going towards Anjuna was named after him in 1996 and the Dalgado Konknni Akademi, (DKA) Panjim named their conference hall after him in 2015, on his 101st birth anniversary. His son, Sally, explains, 'He was a trained violinist but quickly taught himself the trumpet when there was a job available for a trumpeter.'

---

* Goggoddo is typical Indian onomatopoeia, a word designed to evoke a sound (like *khakhataahat* in Hindi for knocking). Godgoddo can mean thunder, but in this case, it came about because some ancestor in the house (most likely my great-uncle Papa John) had a booming voice that could be heard beyond the property.

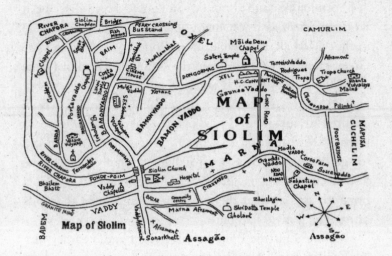

Sebastian D'Cruz's map of Siolim in the 1980s, recreated and
reproduced here with permission

The parochial school was built in 1907 in the compound
of the St Anthony's church to provide education with
an emphasis on teaching Western, classical music. 'The
students, mainly boys, barely in their teens, learnt to play
the violin and knew to read and write music better than they
knew to read and write Konkani and Portuguese,' explains
Sally. The students included legendary Western classical and
sacred music exponent, Joaozinho Carvalho who went on to
be the leader of the popular Goan dance band, 'Johnson and
His Jolly Boys'. Their fame extended across Goa to Mumbai
and it was a big deal if they played at your wedding.*

---

* Mario Cabral e Sa, 'Eminent Goans', Commissionerate of NRI Affairs,
Government of Goa, https://nri.goa.gov.in/eminent-goans/.

Formidable and humble Siolkar, Alexyz has been working relentlessly on many issues since he moved here in the 1970s after growing up in Bombay. Alexyz and the Green Heritage Club initiated the Annual Festival of Plants and Flowers at the St Francis Xavier's School in Siolim in 1992. Alexyz explains, 'It encourages young school children to nurture and love plants. They look forward to it every year and learn so much.' The festival is a mecca for gardening enthusiasts across Goa. I finally went to the festival celebrating its 30th year of inception in 2022. Plants bring me joy, as does the good energy and noise that kids bring. The festival had both.

Siolim holds the dubious distinction and a rather rare honour of having probably the only statue of Ludwig van Beethoven outside of Europe in Pinta Shapai Nivas. The music composer was revered by the family of Diogo Caetano Pinto, who lived till 114 and was addressed as 'Pinta Shapai'.* His great-grandson, Manoel Sousa-Pinto is rumoured to be an eccentric Goan.

In May 1968, he erected a marble bust of his grandfather Pinta Shapai in their ancestral house in Siolim. A family member explains, 'Since there were no pictures of his grandfather, he got the Girgaum sculptor to style the bust based on his and his sisters' good looks.'

After installing the marble bust of his grandfather inside the house, Manoel erected a statue of Beethoven in front of their house for the village that says, 'This immortalizes a giant in art'. The family tried hard to dissuade him from building the statue and pleaded with him to 'use the money

---

* Konkani for grandfather.

Beethoven stands tall in Gausovaddo

to fund a dispensary in the village'. But he was adamant. The dedication reads 'Like every Goan, Ludwig was born with a fiddle in his hand. I thank God that he is now here quite at home in my beloved Goa.'

In 2007, Alexyz was instrumental in setting up the Friends of Beethoven Society, where his college friend, piano virtuoso Marialena Fernandes plays tribute to Beethoven, in front of the Pinta Shapai Nivas. We attended this delightful Noite de Beethoven in Gausovaddo in October 2022 and it was special to see so many trained classical musicians perform in this informal, village locale.

Fact or Fiction?

Alinto Coelho, a civil engineer who is documenting heritage houses in Goa says, 'It is believed that nine Persian men arrived in Goa in the eighteenth century. They converted, became Catholics, took Fernandes as their surname and lived in the village of Siolim. The area they lived in came to be known as Fernandes vaddo.'

How Goa's sweetest mango was born

A juicy Siolim story. The Jesuits are credited with introducing mango grafting in Goa in 1575. As this practice spread across Goa, several prominent families tried grafting on their mango trees. As was the custom, when the Siolim landowners presented these grafted mangoes to the parish priest, he asked for the name. Since this was a new graft, it had no name. The priest then christened these honey-sweet mangoes after the landowner's son—Hilario*—which became Manghilar. The house in Fernandes vaddo stands as a proud witness to the Queen of Goan mangoes —radiant yellow, sugar-sweet and almost fibreless. The harvest is in June at the end of the season. Goa saves the best for last as the Hilario is well worth the wait.

---

* Manga is Portuguese for mango.

I was delighted to learn that the beautiful game which Goenkars are passionate about was introduced to Goa first in Siolim. History and lore both suggest that Father William Robert Lyons, an English Jesuit scholar, arrived in Siolim in 1883 from Udupi to convalesce. Father Lyons fell in love with Siolim and decided to stay on. He saw sports, football in particular, as a crucial part of Christian education, and included it in the school curriculum. Soon, the love for football spread all over Bardez and Salcette. After football was declared the official sport in Portugal in 1893, the Portuguese promoted football in Goa and by the beginning of the twentieth century, there were inter-village tournaments.*

FOOTBALL TRIVIA:

Football was introduced in Goa before Brazil. History and lore suggest that Charles Miller brought football to Brazil in 1894.

More recently, through the 1990s, our neighbour Edward Carvalho was passionate about football. He worked tirelessly to promote and sponsor the Siolim FC (Football Club) and his dream was for them to play in Division 1. He built the stadium in neighbouring Duler, supervising the construction himself. Sadly, he did not live to see it completed, but to honour his legacy, the VIP stand there is named after him.

---

* Marcus Mergulhao, 'When Goa Kicked the Ball before Brazil', *Times of India*, 14 July 2018, https://timesofindia.indiatimes.com/city/goa/when-goa-kicked-the-ball-before-brazil/articleshow/64992700.cms.

Our neighbour Edward Carvalho (1933–98)

Edward Carvalho is also famous for establishing Edricia Farms, a hi-tech dairy farm in Siolim in 1989. The dairy closed down but now his daughter Tanya uses the space to run an organic farm that sells veggies. She also offers farm tours and community activities (art, yoga, dance, ceramics) for kids and adults. In April 2023, she co-hosted Picnique Chic with two of Bombay's top French chefs who recently moved to Goa. They curated a fancy sit-down farm-to-table experience using seasonal, organic fruits, greens and veggies in a plated five-course meal. To cool us down, they plied us with bubbly, wine and gin cocktails. From September 2023 onwards, she organized workshops to promote dying heritage arts like coconut palm weaving, broom and coir rope making.

In October 2023, Tanya collaborated with Alexyz and Erwin Fonseca of Assagao farmers to put together a celebration of the coconut tree, which is a crucial part of Goan identity and heritage. We use every part of it. There were traditional artists demonstrating and teaching palm weaving, broom making, basket weaving, clay moulding and coir rope making. Talented musicians played Konkani classics dedicated to the coconut tree and award-winning artists displayed their coconut tree tributes on canvas and paper. Coconut tree climbers, toddy tappers and coconut shell artists were also celebrated. There were traditional coconut-based foods—dose, samarachi kodi, vonn, jaggery, sannas, toddy bread, barfis, ladoos, as well as coconut coffee lattes, pannacottas and mousses. My favourites were the chutney buns with a shot of toddy. Coco peat, compost for our gardens as well as coconut-based soaps and tonics for our dogs, oils, brooms and scrubbers were all available. The best part was that it brought hundreds of our diverse Siolim community together on a Sunday evening, all for the love of our coconut trees, which are being ruthlessly cut down for construction.

Have You Been to the Siolim Sao Joao Festival?

A highlight on the Goa cultural calendar is the Sao Joao festival celebrated on 24 June every year. Siolim is the capital of the celebrations. As with any feast and our syncretic history, there are many versions of the origin and the interpretation, both religious and indigenous. The Catholic version's genesis for people jumping into wells and ponds has to do with St John the Baptist (Sao Joao). While one hypothesis is related to his moniker of baptizing people (including Jesus) by dunking them in the river Jordan, the other insists it has to do with the same John leaping in his mother Elizabeth's womb when her cousin, the Virgin Mary, visited her.

Indigenous traditions include wearing copels (crowns of fruits, flowers and leaves), similar to the ones worn by single women in parts of Europe for midsummer festivities on the summer solstice (21 June). For centuries, girls and young women have worn these flower crowns as a symbol of purity and fertility. Originally pagan, this ritual was Christianized to include celebrations for the feast of John the Baptist. These flower crowns are fashionable in art (Frida Kahlo), at music festivals (Coachella), in music videos (Beyoncé) and countless social media posts.

Yet another belief is that the festival in Siolim honours new sons-in-law who are invited to the bride's house to celebrate this feast and have to wear a crown of flowers and leaves. He is taken around the village and given sliced fruits—jackfruit, mango slices and local sweets—in the hope that the in-laws will be blessed with a grandchild. The author and historian, Maria de Lourdes Bravo da Costa Rodrigues, in her book *Feasts, Festivals and Observances of Goa* explains: A new son-in-law was on his way to visit his in-laws when he met with an accident and died. Sadly, the villagers did not know him as he had not been introduced to them. As a result, they decided that in the future, they would introduce all-new sons-in-law to the villagers. They chose the feast of St John the Baptist as the occasion to do so.

An old-timer living in Siolim explains, 'We throw sealed bottles of feni into village wells. All the neighbours get together and take turns to jump in, find the feni bottles and drink up.'

In Gausovaddo, for Sao Joao, the devout go in a procession to the crosses in the vaddo, place a copel woven of palm leaves on each cross and pray. Finally, the procession reaches a coconut grove, where one of the faithful wades through waist-deep water to put the copel on the cross. The old-timer continues, 'We enjoy singing special Konkani songs accompanied by the ghumot, *cansaim* (cymbal), *mhadalem* and a trumpet. and shouting "Viva Sao Joao!". Around 4 p.m. we all head for the traditional boat parade. This tradition was revived in 1992 by Alexyz and the Heritage Club and has become a tourist attraction. Elaborately decorated boats enter the mouth of the river in front of the church with great pomp and pageantry. The boatmen get off the festive boats wearing the copels of natural leaves and flowers. They light candles and put garlands of flowers on the cross in front of the church.' The route these boats take up the river is probably the same route that the two Portuguese merchants took with the miraculous statue of St Anthony that the Siolim church legend claims caught the snake. The music concert finale, once highly anticipated, is now criticized for being commercial and overcrowded, having lost its charm.

Both the Hindus and the Catholics in Goa are very religious and celebrate feasts and festivals with great devotion. Every other month, we hear loud music, prayers

Current-day Sao Joao traditional boat parade

and drumming, and see women dressed in beautiful sarees, with aboli and shevanti* fati† in their hair, making rangoli and arranging flowers and leaves on the roads while walking in a procession following a deity in a tempo. As we drive, walk or cycle through Siolim, we often pass a feast and *zatra*.‡

---

* Local flowers.
† Konkani for a string of flowers.
‡ Konkani for pilgrimage festivals.

These zatras usually run for four or five days and beyond the rituals and devotion, were a village marketplace for food, and for farmers, artists and craftsmen to buy and sell their wares. A friend, Amita, explains, 'Nowadays, the zatras have stalls for everyone, games, toys and balloons for the kids, food and clothes.'

The Siolim Zagor

In Siolim, all religions coexist, lighting candles and oil lamps, eating kaddio boddio* and celebrating the Siolim Zagor with the same fervour. Zagor means staying up all night and it is done to please the protector of the village. The story goes that the Zagor is celebrated every year to make sure there is a good harvest. Many Siolkars are certain that if they do not celebrate this festival, their fields will get inundated and their bunds will be destroyed by the Chapora river. In the early twentieth century, it was banned by Portuguese rulers because they considered it a pagan festival. In spite of this restriction, to ensure the Gods remain pleased and continued to bless them with a good harvest, the Hindus and Catholics in the village got together to celebrate it, a tradition that lives on till today.

The Siolim Zagor is held on the day after the Siolim church's Feast of Nossa Senhora de Guia,† on the first Monday after Christmas. The ceremonies combine prayers, songs, skits and dances from Hindu and Catholic traditions

---

* A sweet made for feasts with jaggery and ginger and a sprinkling of sesame seeds. It was also GI-tagged recently.
† Portuguese for 'Our Lady of the Guide'.

in Konkani and Portuguese. A performance starts by invoking the deity Zagorio or Zagreshwar, the Holy Cross, St Anthony (the patron saint of the village) and Saibinn (Mother Mary). This Zagor is a form of Konkani *tiatr** with a difference. A friend, Amita, explains, 'In this dance–drama, actors come onto the stage from the audience and improvise to the accompaniment of a modki band that has the ghumot, madvim and cansalim (cymbals). These tiatrs are crowd-pullers and keep the devotees awake late into the night. It ends around 4 a.m. with a final invocation.'

Every village is associated with one or several ganvdevātas, who are believed to be the founders, ancestors, protectors and members of the village community.† Villagers continue to pray to them to bless the land.

Dovor in Konkani means 'to place on'. The legend goes that travellers walked across villages carrying heavy loads on their heads as there was no transport. These Dovornems (red brick structures) were built so they could temporarily place their loads on them and rest. Once transport came to Goa, these Dovornems were forgotten and are in ruins. My Siolim: The Environment and Heritage Club and Alexyz have been working since 2010 to try and restore them. In April 2023, to celebrate World Heritage Day, the Pinto Rozario family restored the Dovornem originally built by their great-great grandfather Dr Antonio Caitano Souza in 1912 on their property in Portavaddo to help travellers along this busy trade route. The inauguration was a charming village

---

* Tiatr is the most popular form of Konkani musical theatre.
† Alexander Henn, 'Hindu-Catholic Encounters in Goa: Religion, Colonialism, and Modernity' (Indiana: Indiana University Press, 2014), http://www.jstor.org/stable/j.ctt16gz7v6.

Dovornem in Portovaddo

celebration with a blessing, hymns, speeches, folk songs and good Goan food. In her book, *Stories from Goan Houses*, writer and heritage activist Heta Pandit features their iconic Siolim house.

Such a charming tradition to literally and figuratively help to lighten someone else's heavy load—something we can all aspire to do.

Siolim Then—Idyllic Holidays in the 1970s–80s

In the 1970s, my first grand tour deep into my mum's village of Socorro started from the imposing church in the centre, where her parents were married on 4 November 1925. As we made our way around the church, we realized that Mummy was related to someone in every second house. My parents, sister and I went in and out of many homes and were welcomed with open arms everywhere as long-lost cousins (literally). An important stop for us was to meet my mother's godmother. She and her family had been well educated and wealthy but sadly had all taken to the bottle. As we entered their huge imposing house round the corner from the church, I noticed that they had nothing inside, there was none of that grand Goan furniture, no pots and pans but just a bamboo mat on the floor. We had heard whispers that it had all been sold to buy alcohol (a common problem with addiction in Goan families). What I recall most vividly from that evening is that they had nothing left in their living room other than my parents' wedding picture hanging on the wall. It was heart-

My parents, Albert and Biddy Mendonça's,
wedding photo taken on 6 January 1957 in Poona

wrenching and heart-warming at the same time. Typically, on the living room wall in every traditional Goan Catholic home to date, there are studio photographs of weddings, first communions and confirmations. Beyond the immediate family portraits, they often extend to nephews, nieces and godchildren. Traditionally, they were black and white and are now all in colour. My parents' wedding portrait was the last of the relics of a rich past.

Like all good Goans, my time has come for some saudade for a milieu long lost. Over the last fifty-seven years of my life, other than the church and the Chapora River, everything else has changed. In the 1970s, Siolim was truly pastoral—coconut trees and fields, a few grand old houses, hills to climb and backwaters to explore. The iconic St Anthony's church with its legend of St Anthony holding the snake was a landmark.

I have a palpable nostalgia for the summer holidays I spent here in the 1970s and 1980s. Many other Goan families and friends from Pune and other cities, did not have the same luxury of going to their ancestral homes. They had to stay with family friends or in hotels because their homes were in disrepair, sold off, donated, rented, encroached upon or lived in by other members of their extended family and they were not welcome.

A photo of our house taken in 1989

In this context, we knew we were lucky to be able to visit a cosy and rustic house in April–May every year. It would take us a twelve-hour overnight journey from Pune by bus. We would get off at Mapusa and sleepily find our way to Siolim, usually on another bus. Sometimes, if my parents were feeling exhausted or extravagant, we took a cab. We always looked forward to living the village life for a month.

Our house was charming but basic. There was a big, whitewashed cross in front (still is) and our balcao faced the church. Around the house, we had several coconut trees—I remember Daddy saying there were over forty. No road but just a red mud path, no compound walls or gates but densely crowded mango, coconut, chikoo and jackfruit trees, only a handful of old houses and a few communal wells between our house and the church. There were four strategic large laterite stones marking the property that Daddy inspected every time he visited.

From the start of the road, coming from the church, you could almost see our house through the thicket of coconut trees. The tarred road that now brings you from the church to our home and divides our property, came years later. Many friends and family in Goa have suffered the same fate, the road was constructed leaving them with two separate plots on either side. In some tragic cases, train lines and highways have gone through their home and land.

We had no running water, so we used water drawn from the well to cook, clean, wash and bathe. The novelty of pulling water from the well was hugely exciting for us. We had no electricity so we lit candles and little kerosene lamps—*pontis*—after dark. There was no cooking gas so cooking was done over a wood fire in *kunlis*.* The fire was lit at sunset from dried coconut shells, leaves, husks and fronds. The bathroom was a small partition in the far corner of the kitchen, alongside the woodfire boiling the bath water. You had to strategically bend over the low wall to get hot water from the big *bann/hando*† using another *kohso*.‡

---

* Clay pots.
† Konkani for a giant copper pot.
‡ Konkani for a small copper pot.

Despite the heat and humidity at the height of the tropical summer, we would have steaming hot baths before dinner and bed. The water drained from the bath area watered the banana and other plants.

A string of sausages drying

The storeroom attached to the kitchen had a large loft from which hung rows of chillies, onions and garlic. There may also have been fish and sausages drying up there. At the back of the house, there was a separate storeroom. I think it housed the annual supply of rice, coconuts, tamarind, chillies and other produce. Grandpa's diary records that he owned paddy fields behind our house but had sold them as they were hard to manage from Pune. Old-timers in Siolim, who were then children, still talk about him, his house and his fields. They refer to this house as Minshiningher (I am still not sure who was called, referred to, or had a nickname of Minshin as the term implies it was Minshin's home. Did Grandpa or his father or grandfather have a big Poirotesque moustache and so they were called by that nickname?).

The flooring was red oxide, which I wasn't too thrilled with as I wanted the real village experience—cow dung floors like in other homes we visited, including Grandpa

Marshall's (my mum's dad's) house. I took this up with older relatives, till one day, a grand uncle gently told me, 'You are lucky your ancestral house has a red oxide-tiled floor. They are a luxury. People who can't afford them have to use cow dung. Difficult to manage and they smell. You won't be able to sleep on a cow-dung floor.' I quickly shut up and stopped complaining that I was not getting the authentic village experience. There was an enormous bamboo mat rolled out at night and in the afternoon too for the siesta. Each of us was thrown a pillow and a sheet, and every night, we fell asleep to the smells of a woodfire and the sounds of neighbours' dogs barking. We woke up to roosters crowing and the sun coming in through the open windows.

In the northwest, through the fields, taking a shortcut skirting the St Francis Xavier (SFX) school, we walked over to visit Grandpa Jerry every evening. He had moved to St Joseph's Home for the Aged, close by in Porto Vaddo, which was run by nuns from the Sisters of Saint Joseph of Chambery (my aunt and his daughter, Sister Maryann's convent). We enjoyed visiting him and all his friends there in the evenings as they chatted and said the rosary. One strange experience I recall was Grandpa removing our *dixxtt*, which is some sort of ritual to exorcise the evil eye. This was done to protect and ensure you would stay safe and not fall ill even if someone looked at you with an evil eye. I have a vague memory of this practice—he would take a handful of dried red chillies, salt and a crucifix and with his right hand, draw a few circles around us while we said the 'I Believe' and a few Hail Marys. After this, the chillies would be thrown into a fire and with a giant sign of the cross, Grandpa would bless us—another syncretic ritual.

At noon and 6 (or was it 7?) p.m., the church bells pealed for the Angelus prayer. We did not usually pray the Angelus but sometimes had *pez* with a little mango water pickle or kaalchikodi for a morning snack around 10 a.m. In the evening, we said the rosary by candlelight.

We ate a lot of mangoes from our trees, which was one of the attractions of visiting Goa in May. The mangoes were also made into traditional pickles and jams. We had to walk to the Taar right on the Chapora River to get fish and vegetables. The market there remains almost unchanged— sweet old ladies still sit selling fresh seasonal fruit, veggies and grain from their gardens. For everything else, we needed to make a trip to Mapusa.

There were no street names, no house names, fences or gates—salubrious life. We ate fresh fish, prawns, crabs, tisrios, shenanios and khube* made in the delicious Goan way with lots of fresh coconut from our trees. We were very blessed to have kind caretakers who cooked and looked after us when we visited. They managed the house, land and trees for Daddy while he lived in Pune. When it was time to head back, they made us a vat of dodol† and halwa to carry back in baskets.

The toilets require a special mention as they were pig toilets housed away from the main house under a massive old tamarind tree. Not sure about hygiene or science, but it was environmentally friendly as there was instant reusing. Every morning, you headed over with another copper kohso filled

---

* Mussels and clams.
† Goan sweets made with coconut and jaggery, cooked for hours on a slow flame with a dense, delicious gelatinous consistency.

with water as the pig greedily followed you. You climbed in. The door was made of *mollam** so it could fly open if there was a strong breeze. There was a raised hole and you squatted above it. Below, the hungry pig greeted you with a cheerful grunt that was both reassuring and terrifying, but you stoically or desperately got on with your business. I will leave you to figure out how your daily routines became a hungry piggy's breakfast. We had these outdoor toilets till the 1990s. Even after we got married in 1989 and Bharat came to Siolim for the first time, he experienced the piggy loo.

Memories of Mapusa Market

Mapusa was just one bus ride away. We went to the market there to stock up on Goan sausages, cashew nuts, *sola*,[†] mats, brooms, chillies and other goodies to carry back to Pune. Rex Stores was the place to buy the treasured cashew nuts and sausages. There was also a mandatory stop at St Xavier's Café for a snack of some Goan delicacies—puffs and doce[‡] (there are two versions: my favourite version is made with chana,[§] which has a crusty skin and a gooey centre, and the other iteration is made with semolina and coconut). I also remember relishing the falooda[¶] at the Hanuman cold drinks shop, which was refreshing in the ferocious May heat.

---

* Konkani for dried, plaited coconut fronds.
† Konkani for dried kokum.
‡ Goan coconut sweet.
§ Chickpeas.
¶ A sweet, milky, rose-flavoured drink with some chia seeds.

My mum would occasionally visit the jewellers and use the money she saved up to buy typical Goan designs to wear at weddings—coral, cameo or fator (malachite). An important part of Mapusa shopping was to buy those market bags—black, sometimes brown, rexine and sturdy. When my parents shopped with them in the Pune market, they were the envy of their friends and family, who were not able to make a trip to Goa to buy that year's collection.

This makes me think of a special sepia-coloured memory of Mummy and our summer visits to Goa. In Pune, she was a formidable convent school principal dressed in elegant sarees, teaching, mentoring and counselling hundreds of girls over decades. For our holidays in Goa, she carried a few tailored cotton floral dresses to wear for her village life. Sometimes I got lucky and managed a few for my own Siolim summer collection—a different look from my college jeans and kurtis or salwar kameez.

Though we spent most of our time in Siolim, we often ventured out and took buses everywhere. Taxis were very few and unaffordable, and the travel took half the day, but we didn't care—it was an expedition and we had plenty of time. We would wait for the bus at the corner of our road and hail it down when we heard the bus guy call out 'Mapusa, Mapusa, Mapusa' through the door. We would holler back: 'Rao rey, Rao rey!'* and they would stop for us. If we were lucky, we would get a direct bus to Panjim via Calangute. Otherwise, Panjim and everywhere else meant two or three buses—the first to Mapusa and the next to Panjim or another village. The furthest I had ventured was

---

* Konkani for 'Stop!'.

to Old Goa to visit the Bom Jesus Basilica, which was three bus rides away. These buses all still operate with the same rules and you are packed in like sardines—frightening in Covid times. When there is absolutely no place either in the front or the back of the bus, the bus conductor will yell 'phati vos' or 'phude vos' and you are shoved forward or backwards depending on which side the newcomers enter from. The bus smells of stale sweat, fresh fish, dried chillies and other special Goan aromas.

There was always at least one trip to Panjim (to visit my dad's oldest sister and my godmother, Aunty Blanche and her family there); another trip to Assagao, which was remote, isolated, hilly and forested, where my dad had cousins (on his mum's side); and one to Socorro (where both Mummy's parents were from). We would spend the whole day or a few days in each of these places, walking through the fields and climbing the hills and trees. Arrangements were made in advance by writing letters confirming specific dates, impossible to fathom in these times when plans are made and changed every minute with our smartphones.

We would be excited if there was a church feast, anniversary or wedding to attend. Dressed in our Sunday best, we would sweat our way through the celebrations, a long mass in Konkani, followed by a massive Goan lunch (often including a suckling piglet), music and dancing.

Adventures in and around Panjim

Panjim was, and still is, a gorgeous city—one of the prettiest cities I have ever visited. I have very fond memories of just walking along the riverside at Campal, with its majestic rain tree-lined boulevard at sunset. It was magical. We looked forward to eating those melt-in-your-mouth prawn patties at Perfect Bakery (still great and a regular treat) or a nice Goan lunch at Marietta down the road from Aunty Blanche. Some special Goan goodies were bought at the Tea Centre in the Panjim market across the road. Later came Mr Baker, which was a café to sit or pick up some patties or bebinca from. Daddy always made sure he got a liquor permit to carry a couple of bottles of feni back to Pune on the bus. He might even have carried a bottle of that popular Port wine, the sickly sweet Vinicola, to serve with cake at Christmas.

Another adventure was taking a bus to Miramar Beach and yet another bus to carry us further to swim in the cove at Dona Paula—so remote and romantic. An extravagant treat was to eat choris* pao from a hole in the wall there.

One other regular stop was at Uncle Tony's (Grandma's younger brother) in Socorro. It had been the home Grandma grew up in, and Mummy and her seven siblings had spent their summer holidays in that house visiting their maternal grandmother as children. As I wrestle with my own garden, I remember their perfect garden and potted plants, and how lovingly they watered and nurtured them. Aunty Esme was a gourmet cook and Uncle Tony, a raconteur. He would regale us with tales of family history and Goa while she fed us our favourite prawn curry and ukde tandul.[†]

The brand-new restaurant O'Coqueiro in Alto Porvorim was the talk of the town and being invited to eat there was an

---

* Goan sausage, spicy made of pork and vinegar, stuffed in a pig's intestine and dried. Similar to the Spanish and Portuguese chorizo but spicier and tastier.

† Typical Goan unpolished red boiled rice.

exalted, extravagant experience. The only ones who could afford it were 'foreign return' relatives visiting from the Gulf, the UK or Canada or shippies (men who worked on the ship). It was the fanciest place we had ever eaten at. Alto Porvorim was a deserted hill in those days with not even a traffic light in sight—the only landmark was the big water tank opposite O'Coqueiro that you could spot for miles at the top. It has now been dwarfed by the tall structures that have mushroomed around it.

Calangute Beach in the 1970s

Nostalgia for Calangute Beach

The highlight of our summer holiday in the 1970s was the weekend Daddy booked us at the Tourist Hotel in

Calangute and made sure we got rooms overlooking the beach. It was a very Goa feeling—waking up to the sound of the waves, swimming in the sea in the morning and evening and walking on the stunning golden sand beach. Eating the Goa sausage chilli fry at Souza Lobo, right next door to the Tourist Hotel, was a real treat. One evening every year, we walked along the beach to St Anthony's Bar and Restaurant in Baga for a swim and dinner. Baga was pristine and much less busy than Calangute. We swam in the creek and, if it was low tide, crossed over to climb up to visit the imposing Jesuit retreat house on the rocks on the other side of the Baga Creek. My parents believed, that if you walked down Calangute beach in May, you would meet old friends not just from Goa, but also from Bombay, Pune and other cities holidaying here. As I became a teenager, I looked forward to the 'beat shows' with live bands and dances. It was truly exciting if Remo was performing. There was always music in the air and you were kept entertained and awake with guitar jams and sing-songs in and around the Tourist Hotel and on the beach. While we were there, cousins from Panjim would also come to hang out and stay over. My cousin Geralyn often says, 'You remember how one night, all of us seven cousins slept on the sand, under the stars.'

An early morning May memory was watching a humongous catch of sardines coming in off the catamarans. The fisherfolk were throwing it back as the catch was too big and the fish was too small to get them a good price. We had run into our cousins from Bombay who were also staying at the Tourist Hotel. My cousin Lynn writes, 'I still remember when your family and ours spent a few days at

Big catch of fish coming into Calangute Beach in 1972

a tourist hotel in Calangute in 1972 and a whole catch of sardines rolled up on the beach. Our dads brought bags in and your mum cooked them in the hotel room on a portable stove. The taste of how delicious they were still lingers. We had our dog Bobby with us who I used to smuggle in and out of the hotel.'

Walking along Calangute beach in May, you would see older women from the villages dipping their feet and taking their annual seawater bath before buckling down for the torrential rains. The saltwater is therapeutic and ensures good health through the long, brutal monsoon.

Later in the month, our cousins and friends returned the favour and came to Siolim to spend the day or a couple of days with us. More mats and more pillows, more water pulled from the well and heated for baths. Some summers, friends from Pune came with us and those were the best holidays as we had company to play all the time. We would all chat late into the night in the candlelight.

As I am reliving these Goan summer holiday memories spent with my parents, there are a few that I must retell.

One memory is an unforgettable trip to Tiracol in the early 1980s. It was with good family friends, Uncle Nasci and Aunty Thelma, who drove from Madras to Siolim every summer. Uncle Nasci and Daddy knew each other from their days in the College of Engineering in Poona in the late 1940s. That evening, Uncle Nasci drove his ambassador on to the ferries to cross the Chapora River from Siolim and then later again to cross the Tiracol River to get to the fort. Since all of us did not fit in the car, we found a man with a canoe who was willing to take a couple of us across. It was an exhilarating expedition crossing the Chapora in a canoe. (We recently did this in a kayak and a motorboat, also fun though commercial.) We had carried food and drink for our picnic near the Tiracol fort. We swam, ate, drank, sang and danced, returning home late that night. A lasting memory in full colour. So different from today, when we drive across two bridges from Siolim to get to Tiracol in under an hour.

The summer story that always makes me smile was when I was in college and came to Goa in the mid-1980s. We met up again with Uncle Nasci and Aunty Thelma and their daughter Sonya. She took me to Panjim to meet her cousin Nelinha, her bestie Piki and their friends and family there. They showed us the exciting Panjim big city life. There were around ten of us, packed into a tiny Fiat. We drove to distant beaches by day to swim. At night, we went to Miramar and Dona Paula to sing, play guitar and dance. It was truly a blast. The stuff of teenage dreams—beach, music, singing and dancing. As I see the squall that Arambol is today, I recall the day we went there in the 1980s. In our quest for a far, far away beach in 1986 we drove far north, crossing the Siolim ferry. We realized we were probably in pristine Arambol. We tumbled out of the car, hoping to jump into the blue sea to swim. On closer inspection, our young innocent eyes were mortified to see a nudist colony enjoying a game of beach volleyball. Scandalized, we quickly climbed back in and drove onto the beaches of Keri.

Since I am well down this road reminiscing about village life in Siolim, I must go even further back and retell a story Daddy often told us. It was about his holidays to Siolim when he and his sisters were in school and college. They came by train as their father worked for the railways. Daddy always laughed at what we called first-class train travel in our lifetime. 'We travelled first class when we came from school, we had our own first-class separate bogie/compartment that was attached to the regular train. It came with stewards in white gloves who served us soup and the rest of our courses including the pudding. We slept two in a cubicle with our own attached toilet.' Talk about luxury travel. The train brought them to Mormugao. 'We arrived in Goa with our entire household including dogs, staff and cooks. From Mormugao, we took the ferry to Dona Paula. At Dona Paula, we took some sort of carriage/covered bullock cart to the Panjim ferry. From Panjim, we crossed the Mandovi in a ferry to Betim and then took another of those bullock cart-like contraptions with big wheels all the way to Siolim.' After arriving in Goa by train, getting to Siolim took almost a whole day. When they arrived, they unpacked and got settled for their two-month vacation. My guess is these holidays were in the 1930s and 1940s.

Another story Daddy often told was about his Siolim school holidays. One of their dogs regularly chased the pigs in the neighbourhood and one day, finally managed to get a hold of a neighbour's pig. Pigs are quick, beguiling their shape and size but he somehow managed to catch one. The neighbour was not happy. Apologies were made and a price was settled. 'We ended up eating pork roast, vindaloo and sorpotel for weeks,' he said.

When we complained about walking in the heat to the corner to catch the bus to the Mapusa market, Daddy would tell us, 'You are grumbling about walking to the corner, just a few hundred metres from our house to take a bus to Mapusa? We used to walk over the hill to Assagao, meet our cousins Joe and Peter and uncles and aunts, have a cup of tea with them, and then continue to the Mapusa market over the next hill. After doing the marketing for the house here, with the heavy bags, we would walk back again via Assagao, have lunch, lie down in the afternoon, have a cup of tea and then walk back over the hill to Siolim that evening. Sometimes, we stayed over in Assagao and then walked back to Siolim the next morning, bringing some of them along with us. You are complaining about this short walk, we climbed two hills twice a day. There were no buses. We had to walk everywhere.'

Driving from Siolim to Assagao now, when I am stuck in a traffic jam of two-wheelers, four-wheelers, cement mixers and earth movers, all headed for the restaurants, cafes, yoga studios and construction sites, I think of Daddy walking over the same hill in the 'good old days'.

Siolim Now—Angsty Urban-Rural Purgatory

Friends riding over call and say, 'How can you live here? We're currently rattling down your road. It has more craters than the moon!' Goan neighbours believe it is not all bad, 'With all these potholes, there will be less traffic, so let it be. Don't complain.'

In this nouveau semi-urban Siolim, despite all this 'progress and development', there is zero planning, urban or rural. There are shortages of basics like water and electricity, no sewage system and a limited garbage collection process.

Door-to-door dry garbage collection started as recently as January 2020 (after years of lobbying, as the waste was piled up on the sides of the road. In fact, it still is). Garbage was burnt and often still is, which creates carcinogenic smoke. The wet garbage—kitchen waste along with all the leaves that fall—we mulch and compost to use in our garden. Others try to do the same, while many continue to burn dry leaves. Solid waste management and segregation are rudimentary here—there is no regular, organized safe disposal of either biowaste or e-waste. Covid created so much biowaste and also revolutionized our overdependence on technology, which in turn added to the e-waste. Batteries (which we have too many of) are dangerous and I never know how to dispose of them safely. The solid waste treatment plant set up in Saligao in 2016 is already struggling to cope with the volume. Then there is the horror of landfills—unsustainable and unattainable, given the rising cost of land. You cannot imagine how much glass waste there is across the village and the state, as it is not picked up regularly nor is it recycled.

Another unforgivable crime is broken bottles. You often see tourists roll down the window and chuck a bottle out of a moving car—hazardous and callous. Even more nauseating is when they crawl out of cars, engine running and pee on the side of the road. They spit too. As I look at the road in April, it is dark blue from the juicy, fallen jambul fruit and chequered with red putrid, paan stains.

I am always grateful to rag pickers in Siolim who provide invaluable public service by picking up the mounting piles of garbage. They originally worked on the Baga–Calangute–Candolim beach belt, helping the shack owners collect the plastic and glass waste and keep the beach clean, since the local government did not provide these basic civic services. Over the years, as tourism and migration have spread across the North, rag pickers have started collecting, sorting and recycling the waste, while living in inhumane conditions and facing discrimination themselves.

As I walk Haruki in my vaddo most evenings, when I look down, I see garbage—plastic, empty bottles of beer, water or coke, chips, chocolate and tobacco packets. If I look up, I see a thick canopy of old mango and coconut trees. And when I look around at eye level there are earth movers and cement mixers.

We pay a house tax annually to the panchayat in April every year and in recent years, there has been an additional small fee for garbage collection. As with everything, I hear contrarian opinions about this fee. Aunty Sandra says, 'So expensive! Now we also have to pay for this garbage collection when we were just burning it earlier,' while young Dhruv explains, 'Our house tax is only Rs 1500 for the whole year, dude. We live in a community of eight stand-alone three-bedroom villas. If the panchayat charged us more, they could manage all these other services like garbage, water and streetlights better. In Mumbai, we paid Rs 10,000 a quarter to our society and we had a poky, two-bedroom apartment. Goa is insane, man. So cheap.'

Our water supply is regular only because we have a well. However, it is no longer safe to drink water straight from the well without purification as the groundwater is toxic from too many soak tanks/pits. A soak pit, also known as a soakaway or leach pit, is a covered, porous-walled chamber that allows wastewater to slowly seep into the surrounding soil.* The solid waste is stored in the septic tank. The contaminated water from the septic tank floats to the top and is filtered into an adjoining soak pit. The soak pit then further filters the water and releases it into the groundwater table. The septic tank needs to be regularly drained of the solid waste it holds. Most of us who have lived in cities

---

* Soak Pits', Swiss Federal Institute of Aquatic Science and Technology, https://sswm.info/factsheet/soak-pits, last accessed 16 October 2023.

have no understanding of how to manage the bacteria in this ecosystem without chemicals so that the solid waste biodegrades. In November 2021, after ten years of having this extension, we had to empty our septic tank and needed to organize septic tankers from Panjim. Buildings and villa communities need them to be drained far more regularly. It is an unpleasant event with the stink. Unfortunately, till there is a proper sewage system in the villages, with the exponential increase in construction, there are a growing number of septic tanks and soak pits.

In October 2023, many of the popular beaches were infested with disease-causing pathogens making them unsafe to swim in. According to the latest data released by the Central Pollution Control Board (CPCB) in July, the presence of faecal coliform indicates that the water has been contaminated with faecal matter from humans or animals. This comes from the many shacks, hotels and homes that pump out untreated or partially treated raw sewage or domestic waste into the water.*

In Siolim, we are only slightly better off than some villages. A friend who lives in Alto Porvorim laments, 'We have no water in the wells nor do we get regular water supply. Our society depends on a weekly water tanker delivery.' This is another unethical business nexus between the builders, the panchayat officials, and the bore well and tanker delivery owners. In the summer of 2023, we struggled to water our garden as the well was running

---

* 'Goa's Beach Waters Infested with Disease Causing Pathogens: Data', The Goan EveryDay, 13 October 2023, https://www.thegoan.net/goa-news/goa%E2%80%99s-beach-waters-infested-with-disease-causing-pathogens-data/104741.html.

low and the water supply was irregular, and parts of our lawn dried out as a result. With dwindling water resources and fierce monsoons, we need to urgently plan to harvest rainwater and store it for the summer. With all this concrete construction, the rainwater has nowhere to go so there are floods during the monsoons while the water table is running dry in the summer as it is not getting recharged despite the fierce monsoons.

Across Goa, cell phone network coverage is patchy and online banking or shopping transactions are always stressful and dicey. You may not have a cell phone signal just when you need the one-time password (OTP) to complete the transaction within the deadline. With almost all our financial transactions being done digitally, this leads to a hop, step and jump dance routine—swinging your hands and hanging out of your balcony looking for a tiny spot of connectivity or rushing to one corner of your garden for the pin to complete the transaction. The internet here is fibre optic, but more erratic than stable as there are far too many disruptions and outages due to road work, trees falling or being cut down. Also, since the router requires electricity, it becomes tough to work seamlessly.

No Reliable Public Transport

The buses to villages are slow and infrequent, making travel for the average Goan extremely difficult. Many relatives say, 'We can't come over to visit you, Michelle. On Sundays, buses are even more irregular and on weekdays the last bus is at 7 p.m.' Most visitors take taxis. When they are here on holiday, they often call and say, 'We will just Uber over' or

'I will walk to the corner and hail a cab or rickshaw.' When we say there is no Uber or Ola or any kind of car-hailing app and there are no cabs or rickshaws on the corner, we are met with disbelief. 'How can it be? What do you mean?'

No taxis are standing on street corners in Siolim or most villages. The ones that are found outside popular restaurants, bars, hotels and tourist places do not use a meter and insist on being hired at a price they decide. There is very little room for negotiation. Tourists have to engage a full-time overpriced cab for their trip to get around Goa.

Many male village Goans drive taxis. It is their source of a secure livelihood. The income was historically seasonal, so they charged whatever they could get. The taxi drivers seem to have the power of their votes. They have so far blocked all private automated apps and are not cooperating with the government-sponsored and locally-developed taxi-hailing app 'GoaMiles' but prefer to maintain their autonomy so they can work only when they want. They don't want the apps to tell them where and when they need to pick up a fare. There is also a not-so-secret North–South divide. You cannot take a north Goa taxi to south Goa and vice versa. Goa Miles, I understand, works better from the airport or at the more touristy places but not so much in Siolim—a few friends who have taken it here have not been able to get one to go back. At both the airports, with overpriced cabs also comes complete chaos. However, if you have the money but no time, the new Mopa Airport is now offering a chopper that drops you to your luxury hotel.*

---

* Anu Sharma, 'Taj Exotica Gets Helicopter Connectivity from Mopa Airport of Goa', Mint, 9 February 2023, https://www.livemint.com/

Whenever I take a taxi from the airport, the drivers try to sell me some seedy shacks and bars to go to. When I say I live here, I have been told, 'These outsiders are coming from Karnataka and taking our business. You must vote for our Goa Revolutionary Party to save our Goa.' He does not listen when I say, 'They have my name on their list of people they do not want to vote in Goa. Like all migrants, they don't want me on the voter list.' The taxi drivers speed and overtake so dangerously that I am never sure whether to listen to their sermons on politics or say a few Our Fathers and Hail Marys to reach home safely.

I have taken an Uber from Bombay to Pune for just over Rs 2000, which is approximately 150 km and takes over three hours. I pay the same amount from my home in Siolim to the Dabolim airport, which is about 45 km and takes an hour. If you are here for a brief holiday, you can spring for the cab, but for those who live here, taxis are an occasional extravagance. With slow and unreliable buses and unaffordable taxis, an old aunt says, 'We go out only once a month.'

Given the long distances, high taxi fares and smartphones with Google Maps, self-drive cars and scooters have become very popular. Novice scooter riders are wobbly and unsteady and can't control their scooters. They ride into you and through traffic lights. For self-drive car hires beyond the Swifts, the latest is the macho, fuel-guzzling, open-top Thars that you can sit, stand, preen and pout in while driving around posing for selfies to prove how much you

companies/news/taj-exotica-gets-helicopter-connectivity-from-mopa-airport-of-goa-11675956519974.html.

Grid-locked traffic on Siolim streets

are enjoying your Goa holiday, causing chaos on the roads, endangering commuters and dog walkers.

My friend, Priya, says, 'My neighbour from Mumbai moved over the pandemic and was ecstatic to be living in such a remote village, surrounded by fields. Getting away from it all. But when things opened up and they could venture out, they realized there were no reliable buses. After living their whole life in Mumbai, they did not know how to ride a scooter or drive a car. They moved back soon after with their bag and baggage. Maybe Goa is not so affordable to live in after all?'

Goa also offers pilots—motorcycle taxis for one person riding a pillion. Though they are efficient, they are not cheap or safe, given the roads and traffic. Historically, pilots have been popular as a way of getting out of your village home. I remember listening to aunts of yore talking about their friendly neighbourhood pilot. Aunty Matty would say, 'You know I have Sailesh here—he comes every Friday and takes me first for mass and then to Mapusa market. I do all my marketing there, go to the bank, have lunch and come home.' The only other place I have taken motorcycle taxis is in the *sois* (streets) of Bangkok.

Traffic Chaos

In modern-day Siolim, motorbikes, cars, buses, tractors, earth movers and water tankers are all fighting for space on our tiny village roads.

I no longer leave my gates open as I am afraid that my dogs will run after a stray cat, dog or cow and get hurt by a reckless motorcyclist or speeding driver in that split second. On weekends and during holidays, the traffic is backed up beyond our gate as everyone in their cars, SUVs, scooters and motorbikes are headed to or from the beach. When I do venture out, I hold my breath as one oversized tourist bus tries to cross another huge water tanker on a very precarious village road, inching their way past each other. This delicate operation takes thirty minutes while impatient two-and four-wheel drivers, locals, foreigners and tourists honk, overtake and create absolute mayhem. Does anyone who honks incessantly honestly believe it helps to clear a traffic jam? An old Siolim resident complains, 'There is no room on our tiny, tight, windy and rural roads for the volume of traffic in 2023. Where will all the people from the blocks of flats, luxury homes, row houses, hotels and villa rentals drive and park? Congested roads and chests with all these vehicles belching pollution? How will we survive?' The traffic has brought road rage and aggression. The sleepy, old, polite village ways are gone. If you take twenty seconds too long to take a turn, you will be screamed and honked at. The levels of honking and frustration continue to mount, causing angst, chaos and noise pollution.

You won't find the police managing traffic at blocked junctions, which is where they need to be. Instead, they prefer to congregate at key spots and fine tourists driving without a licence or a helmet and/or going through a one-way, all culpable crimes as long as they give receipts. Our dependence on Google Maps helps them as it does not show the many 'no entry' roads. As a result, tourists unanimously trust Google Maps over big bold road signs and are unfortunately fined by the waiting police force.

If the cops are unscrupulous, I do not have strong enough swear words in my vocabulary to describe our politicians. Goa regularly votes anti-incumbent because of the civic chaos, corruption and profiteering rife across the state. No matter who we vote for, somehow the same party is back in power. During every election campaign, local politicians solemnly swear to fiercely protect our beloved land. They even take oaths to all the Gods one can find in Goa, crossing communal lines right up to the ones on Olympus, to stay with the same party and fulfil their election promises. Within a few weeks of getting chosen as the government, they sell their soul to the devil, cross the floor and go back to being the same governing party as before. Since we were six adults voting in the last state and panchayat elections, we were visited and wooed by all the candidates with their elaborate manifestos and promises on how they would work for us and our interests giving us reliable water, electricity and governance.

The Road to Progress

In 2005, when we got serious about restoring and extending this house, we started looking for contractors, which turned out to be hard, as it was at the beginning of this construction boom. Contractors weren't interested in restoring an old house when they were busy building their million-dollar projects—resorts, hotels and gated communities to sell the Goan dream. In 2008, when I needed tiles, taps and toilet bowls, I had to drive to Mapusa or Panjim. The same held true for curtains, fridges and washing machines. When I needed to open a bank account, my only choices were the nationalized Corporation and State Bank. Today, every other large private Indian bank has a branch in Siolim and has a special offer or once-in-a-lifetime deal. Lockers (bank safe deposit boxes) are elusive and I was relieved to find one in the two-year-old IndusInd bank right here in Siolim.

By 2020, mobile phone shops were ubiquitous. Now, the streets are lined with stalls selling kitschy kurtas, synthetic sarees, plastic pots, pans and jewellery, and there are restaurants, shacks, bakeries, halwais, toy shops and supermarkets. AJ, the first supermarket opened in Siolim and run by women, deserves a special shout-out. We also have a row of pool installation and maintenance shops as well as huge paneer and peda chain stores.

I can buy a fancy mirror, wardrobe and orthopaedic mattress, and find a mechanic to fix or service every kind of kitchen appliance, car, scooter, cycle, television or air conditioner.

The pandemic brought plenty of chemists across Siolim. After the pandemic, we seem to have more pharmacies than wine shops. For animals, there are pet pharmacies and accessory stores and an impressive philanthropic animal rescue centre, Welfare for Animals in Goa (WAG), started and run by the magnanimous Atul Sarin. The centre looks after strays—cattle, monkeys (my nemeses), dogs, cats and birds. The rescue centre wasn't here when we adopted our two indies, Rusty and Roo, and realized that even in the benevolent animal adoption world, girls are often discriminated against and male pups are preferred.

An important Siolim-based philanthropic initiative that provides invaluable service is the Holy Cross Indo-German Techno Centre, which is a technical institute and nursing bureau. It was started by a German, Rudolf Schwartz, in the 1990s and has been growing since. They provide critical home nursing and caregiving for the ailing and ageing, which has seen a rising demand across Goa, for those who can afford it.

A DTDC courier outpost with the good old Siolim Post Office facilitates express parcel service. We have Konkan Cordage, a coir factory, that uses the coconut husk to make and sell rope, mats and other coconut products. It also sells the very useful cocopeat that is much needed in gardening. In case you want a haircut or a makeover, there are plenty of beauty salons for both men and women to choose from as well as gyms and co-working spaces. You can hear loud dance music in the season from Siolim's Riverbanks, our very own wedding venue right on the river. If I ever decide I am old enough or cool enough to get a tattoo, there are two imposing tattoo parlours, each spread over two floors. Importantly, if you need any dental work—extractions, cleaning, filling or getting a tooth implant—you can do it right here at our very own state-of-the-art Sofiya dental facility. As a family, we have great faith in the Siolim public health centre. They have sorted us out with our many emergencies—dog bites, jellyfish stings, kitchen and scooter accidents as well as Covid vaccines, testing and treatment.

In early 2022, Siolim got its very own D'Cruz petrol pump—a milestone. Many young women work at this pump, efficiently handling the traffic, filling up petrol or diesel and accepting payment. A visiting friend dismissed my local intel and said, 'We just buy from the roadside in refilled plastic bottles and hope it doesn't blow up.' Another strange Goa phenomenon—you are on holiday and so cough up the premium for the convenience.

As vegetables and fruits come from across state borders, there was a critical shortage during the first unplanned lockdown. These have so many pesticides that they are believed to be responsible for the high rates of cancer in the state. Most of the plants in the nurseries today come from Pune—also rumoured to be pumped with chemicals, they are required at scale for the landscaping needs of new constructions. The rivers are polluted—originally from mining waste and now with untreated sewage and industrial waste. Additionally, plastic pollution is so serious that microplastics have found their way into fish and seafood, turning marine life toxic. For a fish-eating community such as ours, this is horrific.

Local, Indian and International Food Choices

In some ways, the lockdown gave Goan food a comeback opportunity. Home cooks and caterers started using Facebook and WhatsApp groups to share their homemade delicacies, found an appreciative audience and were able to make ends meet. However, it landed a devastating blow to the entertainment and hospitality industry. We met talented musicians and bartenders delivering our food as they worked as Swiggy and Zomato delivery guys to survive. Locals looked for alternate ways to earn a living—delivering fish, meat, fruit and veggies at wholesale rates. The poder's horn was appropriated by many selling their wares door-to-door, making for a loud and noisy village life.

An array of small shops has sprung up across the village. The growing number of chicken and mutton shops are stereotypically run by the migrant Muslim population. Similarly, the many small grocery stores that my parents would refer to as 'baniyas' are also stereotypically run by the migrant Marwari, usually the Rajasthani community. They also own the many lighting and sanitary stores we now have all over Siolim.

Today, we are living in this post-modern, part-rural-part-urban twilight-zone world. International chains like Baskin Robbins, KFC and Dominos opened in Siolim. Indian food brands such as Amul and Monginis as well as the Goan Navtara and Carusid all have outposts in Siolim.

As I sit here in 2023, Swiggy or Zomato (food delivery apps) deliver dosas or bagels and cream cheese or almond croissants (my favourite) to my door. I have a choice of pizzas, pastas and burgers at any time. On the weekends, if I feel like having Asian food, I can choose between dim sum, ramen, bibimbap, poke or khow suey bowls and end with salted caramel ice cream, passionfruit cheesecake or pasteis de nata for dessert. For teatime, there are so many varieties of brownies, that at this point it's easier to pick one instead of my favourite, bebinca. For an evening snack, I can walk to the *bhelwalla* or pau bhaji guy at one end of the road or to the shawarma or smoothie guy at the other end or wait for the poder who now also brings samosas and cream rolls to my door. We have a *khau galli* that comes alive every evening with a long line of gaddos* and food trucks offering a quick Goan snack—ros omelette,† choris pao, cutlet pao‡ as well as pulled pork burgers.

Give us this day, our daily pao, cream rolls and samosas

---

* Konkani for cart.
† Goan dish—chicken xacuti gravy with an omelette.
‡ Popular Goan street food, choris pao, has Goan sausage stuffed in a pao, cutlet pao has a slice of beef or chicken deep fried in a batter and stuffed in a pao, it also may have a little gravy, tomato sauce and some chopped cabbage.

If you are vegan, like my son Kunal, there are plenty of options for spreads, cashews, almonds or coconut butter, cacao jam, soya delights, and lots and lots of peanut butter. For my morning coffee, I must decide which kind of coffee roast and bean I feel like drinking, Italian (Moka pot), french (French press), cold brew steeper or pour over. If I want to step out, there are so many cafes, coffee shops and co-working spaces that I am spoilt for choice. Fortunately, there is always the option of a good Goan breakfast—bhaji pao, buns and fried chilli.

It is impossible to keep up with the restaurants that are springing up post-pandemic. End 2022 saw our very own fine dining spot, right on our backwaters—after New Delhi and New York, the team from Indian Accent, which is listed as India's number one restaurant, opened an outpost in Siolim, serving nouvelle South Indian food. My neighbours grumble: 'Have you been there Michelle? We have heard it is very expensive. Only for tourists and outsiders, not for us Goans.'

The Many Siolims and Goas Today

On a September 2021 Sunday morning, trying hard not to let my latest linen loungewear look too crumpled from my breezy drive over, I walked into an Assagao brunch. I'm stopped at the imposing entrance by a sweating security guard. 'Sorry bhaiya, where can I park?' He looks surprised to see a dishevelled me. Disentangling my cream kaftan and knotted, unruly, salt-and-pepper hair, I approach the entrance. The door swings wide open and Laxmi has a big welcoming smile. 'Namaste madamji. *Kaise ho? Bahoot dino baad* [How are you? Been so long]'. 'Been travelling. Missed you too. How's Neena?' '*Sab theek hai, aapke intezar mein baithi hai* [All good, she's waiting for you].' I rush through the familiar coiffured garden, up the sweeping staircase and into the modern balcao. I go flying into Neena's arms, air-kissing, 'Finally! What will you drink? Bahadur can fix your favourite feni cocktail.' I accept the sweating drink, umbrella et al. and sink into a lounger, overlooking the inviting infinity pool. I nod away watching birds, guests and babies jump in and out.

Reclining there, semi-comatose, I think of Aunty Lourdes, a few doors down. I had to shout, scream, bang and do a little dance before she could hear and slowly amble up her imposing balustrade to open the barricaded gate tied with blue nylon rope. I admired her bright yellow croton hedge and her pink mussanda* in full bloom, while she wrestled with the rust. 'How are you, my girl? Thanks so much for dropping in to see me. So lonely here, no? All alone in this old house, can't go anywhere with this Covid. Anna and Chris won't let me. They are both out—one in Canada, one in New Zealand. Anna calls me every day on this WhatsApp so I can see her babas. Things are so bad for her now in Canada, both her babas at home, plus she has to do her office work and her housework. What to do? Can't help. Big house she has there you know, basement with that big Smart TV something. Deck and lawn and all. She only mows the lawn. Her husband Victor has no time. He works in a restaurant so has those shifts. Never home. You know restaurants are working, delivering food even with this Covid business. How are you managing living in our Goan village my girl? So hard must be for you after living in London and all?'

I hold on to her as we lumber down the many stairs to her crumbling old home with a wrap-around balcao. I remember the deep well at the back of the house and memories of that huge, comforting tamarind tree flood back. Chuckling to myself about the summers spent sitting

---

* The mussaenda pink bushes are evergreens in the Rubiaceae family that bloom all year-round. While the pink/salmon are the most popular in Goan gardens, red, white and yellow blooms on these bushes are also seen.

in the shade sharing secret crushes with cousins, I hope that old trees don't have ears or memories.

I watch Aunty Lourdes open the imposing front door in her flowery green housecoat. And then in her dark kitchen, struggling to find the lighter for the gas, she shuffles over to a fridge, also well past its prime, for some milk. Aunty Lourdes then stoops into the antique meat safe and scrounges around for some Marie biscuits to go with the tea. She lays them out for me on a stained melamine plate on top of her now yellowing, crochet tablecloth that covers her antique, wooden and ornate kitchen table.

As I accept the milky-sweet chai and biscuits, I smile to myself about my chat with Ravi, who I ran into on the way over to Aunty Lourdes. I had stopped at the popular French bakery for my fix of their mouth-watering almond croissants—I felt guilt-ridden but every bite of the 20,000 calories was worth it. Tying up his man bun and wiping sweat onto his vest, Ravi asked, 'You're Kunal's mom, right? I see you here every Sunday. Live around?' 'Not far, in Siolim.' 'Hey Siolim, that's cool, man. I live in Kensington Gardens. You know where it is?' I spot the tattoo on his forearm—thinking 'another Japanese character'. 'Awesome yaar, overlooking this huge paddy. Loving this monsoon man. Such heavy rain. So many cool places here dude. I've also seen you over at Uddo, drinking beer, taking in the sunset.' I flinch, caught red-handed, again, another guilty pleasure. He doesn't notice: 'I'm never going back to Bengaluru, bro. All my friends have moved here. I love Goa! It is all just amazing here.'

As I leave the French café, I wave at Andrea, who I recognize from my yoga class, sitting at her regular table.

One hand holding her coffee cup, the other smoothening down her straw blond hair. 'Hey Andrea, what happened to your motorbike, riding a scooter these days?' She rolls her eyes and shrugs. Andrea stops for coffee and a breather between feeding stray cats and dogs and her Sunday Ashtanga class. I wonder if I should go back now that the classes are face-to-face again.

I say hi to Firoza, who I know from her small cotton clothing store and cafe, as I walk out. She pours her heart out: 'So tough managing my restaurant and shop. Things are getting so expensive. People from Delhi buying up everywhere. We came to Goa to escape that big city life and it's followed us here. Struggling to pay all the bills and find staff now.' Another acquaintance, Aarti, in her flowing indigo skirt, big kohl-rimmed eyes and calming aura blows a kiss at me, saying: 'I have found my tribe here. I moved for conscious living. Slow food, slow fashion, slow travel. We need to think about what we eat, wear and how we travel and consume to save our planet. Look at what's happening here in Assagao, you must come for our protest to the panchayat.' I nod vigorously in agreement. Entering the café, I watch someone staggering in while taking a long pull of whatever he is smoking. His glazed, sleep-deprived eyes lead me to conclude that he is now going home after his all-night partying and needs a cup of coffee. He must be a regular here, as the girl at the counter looks at him and asks: 'Your double espresso, Sergei?'

Seated at the corner table is Azhar, an acquaintance from Mumbai who just moved here. Dressed in a button-down white cotton shirt with AirPods in his ears, twiddling a pen in his right hand, he is peering at Excel sheets and talking animatedly to many people in boxes on his laptop screen. Deep in discussion, he doesn't see me. As I leave, I am almost knocked over by two kids in their twenties, gesticulating wildly, 'Now that you are living here bro, you have to taste this bhaji pao, dude. It's the real authentic Goan breakfast, amazing. Real local. They have this bhaji with some mushrooms and potato, it's called some patal bhaji dude. It's to die for. At first, I was hating on it, who wants to eat pau bhaji for breakfast in Goa? But it's not like what you get in Mumbai. You have to try it, man. It's what these real, local Goans eat here. It's at some Cafe Bhosale in Panjim. My cousin who cycles with a group of real Goans there, went with them. He took me.'

In Siolim and Goa, today lives a curious, eclectic mix of Goans and outsiders.

I hate stereotypes, but here I am putting people in collections, categorizing and cataloguing. My observations are all based on shameless generalizations, and I am creating caricatures and composites to make a point. I know there are many layers and that there is no black and white. All these different 'types' live close to each other with very different lifestyles all down the road. I wonder if the Chapora ever meets across the many Goas.

Here are the different people who call my street and Goa home:

- The Goans who have always lived here. They never left. A few from the family may have been in the Gulf or on the ship and returned. Some from their family have immigrated to Portugal, the UK, or the New World (USA, Canada, Australia or New Zealand), but the old-timers still live here in their ancestral homes. Around them, they have extended or built modern houses or flats for their growing families. These extensions also include rooms, studios and furnished apartments that are rented out to tourists, both short- and long-term. These are above, around or across the road from the original homestead. The people know the local history, lore and traditions, celebrate all the feasts, and know what to cook and when to cook it. They also lovingly tend to their gardens, trees and plants and keep busy with year-round do-it-yourself (DIY) projects in their homes and gardens. They are both creative and handy and have a strong aesthetic sense. Regulars at the tiatr and other religious and cultural festivals in the church compound, their conversation is about the local produce, football, feasts, scams and politics. They listen to loud 1970s music, typically Carpenters, and run tourism-related services—taxis, scooter rentals, restaurants or catering.

- Returning Goans: Some bought land or houses or flats and have been moving into the vaddo since the 1980s. Others, like me, returned to build, restore and extend their ancestral homes. They are well-adapted to village life, ride scooters or drive cars for their chores and love their music. Some run small home businesses. Many live here full-time. Others live in the bigger cities or Gulf countries but come regularly for routine maintenance, monsoon repair and readiness of their house, feasts and holidays. They have sunk their roots, adapting easily to village life and enjoying gardening, gossip and feni.

- The older, long-term 'foreigners', typically English, French, Italian and German, who have lived here forever.

Can you hear the Carpenters playing Top of the World?

I'm not sure if they were original hippies who never left or the newer kind looking for yoga and peace. Most ride their scooters; some own local businesses making clothes, scarves or jewellery; some run restaurants, bars, fromageries, pizzerias or gelatos; do yoga, play music and volunteer with different NGOs, usually animal rescues. They live closely in tight-knit communities and meet regularly for movie, book or game nights, thrifting, or organizing clothes swaps.

- Those who are 'finding themselves' or running away from themselves. Not just anxious millennials but people aged anywhere up to seventy-five, who have many interests and usually work in those interests, running local sustainable businesses or cafes. They're people who may also play or create music, indulge in pot, yoga or both. They talk about how happy they are to have escaped the big city life, with the variation being the city they are escaping. It could be Mumbai, Pune, Bengaluru, New York, London, Paris, Toronto and the list goes on . . .

- Musicians, who have moved to Goa for the long history of Western music here. To have the opportunity to learn from veterans, jam with each other and local legends and have plenty of places to perform (pre- and post-pandemic as there was no work during the pandemic). There is an evolving pay-as-you-go entrance and cover charge in a few places that offers more opportunities for musicians to earn a living in Goa now.

- The creative cohort: Chefs, writers, artists, designers, filmmakers, photographers and architects who think Goa has more creative space. Some have school-going children or are home-schooling their children. They are looking to make a better life away from big cities for themselves and their families. They look for progressive schools, try to lead a more sustainable lifestyle and usually live in a community close to like-minded folk. Each person is committed to their art form and hosts community events. They meet at gallery openings to discuss their love for Goa, its culture, freedom and the inspiration it affords.

- Retired folks: Goans and outsiders who have moved here for the next stage of their lives, for a quieter lifestyle and a slower pace. They sometimes consult occasionally in the fields they formerly worked in and travel for business and leisure. They also enjoy gardening, live music, restaurants and the beaches that Goa offers.
- Entrepreneurs: Many who are running luxury lifestyle stores, restaurants, small or medium-scale enterprises. There are many start-ups including incubators and investors, who are working to support local and grassroots movements in Goa. Also, there's a new breed of individuals working in tech, environment and gin industries, whose job titles are truly aspirational— everyone is a CEO, co-founder, evangelist, curator, sometimes all four, all under thirty. Many are 'serial entrepreneurs' with some sort of American accent, who spout jargon and tech lingo, and claim they are on the verge of a multi-million-dollar investment, and their company is soon going to be a unicorn.*
- Activists: Those working with NGOs, funding grassroots organizations committed to preserving Goa's rich biodiversity and fighting for other socio-political and human rights causes.
- Working professionals: Doctors, engineers or those working for the government, banks or industrial estates. They have moved here for work and their relationship with Goa is no different than if they were transferred to any other city—it's just another place to live and

---

* Companies with a valuation of $1 billion without being listed on the stock market. This is the dream of any tech start-up.

work. They rent a flat and usually drive a scooter or car to work every day (as the public bus service is still unreliable, and in Covid times, non-existent).

- Russians: They live here and have been working from home (before Covid). Some run local businesses, typically catering to fellow Russians. A few have married Goans and live here with their families. Their kids go to local schools. You meet them at the traditional Goan celebrations in the vaddo, in the village shops and at the beach. The war in Ukraine has upended their lives. They don't know if they can ever go home. Ukrainian refugees have also moved to Goa since the war started in 2022.

- Luxury (Vanity) homeowners: Non-Resident Indians (NRIs) and High Net worth Individuals (HNIs) and 'those Delhi people' who have bought homes here to add to their collection of farmhouses, houses in the hills and London (Kensington more specifically) flats. They bring their friends with them and spend time visiting others in their circles who also have homes here. Their conversation revolves around who else has/ is buying/building a home in Goa, landscaping, art and architecture, designer wear and handbags, property law and the current property values, the hassle of recruiting and retaining domestic staff, the latest boutiques, galleries and restaurants to shop/eat in, and of course, international travel. They have little to no interaction or interest in Goa or Goan culture other than food, where they show a passing interest in the occasional vindaloo, balchao or xacuti.

- Investment homeowners: A mix of Goans and outsiders. Those who have invested in a second home and are typically professionals from Mumbai, Gurgaon, Bengaluru, Hyderabad, Ahmedabad, Pune, Dubai and Singapore. They own a flat or row house in a gated community and visit for only about a week or two in the year, usually around the school breaks—summer, Diwali and/or Christmas-New Year period—with their friends and head to the beach, shacks, live music events and restaurants.

- The rich and famous (celebrities): These include movie stars, sports persons, designers, industrialists and other millionaires in vogue. They have homes and live lifestyles you read about in magazines and watch on *Lifestyles of the Rich and Famous* (1984–96). They travel with a posse, oh sorry, squad, their famous friends and sometimes on private planes (even more so in Covid times).
- Urban, middle-class, single women as well as the LGBTQIA+ community during various life stages who move to Goa for safety and acceptance or to start over.
- The Covid city escape crew (pandemic migrants): Many young and not-so-young people who came here to work from home for the pure air and lifestyle. Since they work remotely, they stitch together teams from across the country and the world and enjoy the joys of Goan village living. Most are here for a work–life balance and to avoid burnout. They now travel to the big cities when they have work but continue to live in Goa.

Many have moved with young and school-going kids and are looking for progressive schools in Goa, beyond the government and religious ones in the cities and villages. The growing trend for international schools spreading across India has also reached Goa and these schools have made it more attractive for families with young children to move here. In October 2023, Twitter (now X) reported South African cricket legend Jonty Rhodes moved to South Goa and enrolled his kids in an international school where our daughter, Divya, taught from 2021–2022.

Training wheels for the wee ones

Who Does Goa Belong To?

We all seem to live in our own little bubbles, cheek by jowl as every inch of space on this road and leading off this road is claimed. We sometimes overlap in local supermarkets and banks (united in our grumbling about the slow service), vets and animal shelters (unanimous in our humanity for animals) or yoga classes (where we collectively feel the energy in our communal 'Om' chanting). We also bump into each other in our dancing queen avatars at that late-night frantic salsa, bachata and jive sessions as we swirl across different locations in the north depending on the dance and the day.

Goa offers a common love—everyone knows everyone as there is always some connection. The world is much too small. Within each of these communities and ecosystems, paths cross. I and everyone else here meet people from previous lives—from school, college or work. I have an additional complication as they could be related or connected to me. My young friend Leela says honestly: 'There is always some drama here. People are forever falling out, either their business or romantic partnership does not work out. I can't afford to take sides in a fight, man. If I pick a side, I will have no friends left and no places to go in Goa.'

In the village, you need to keep your friends close and your neighbours closer. Everyone looks out for everyone. They know when you walk your dog, who your dog attacked or which dog attacked him. You could be asked:

'When you came? Which flight? You drove from Mumbai?'

'Who visited you last night? They came in a white Maruti. Left very late.'

'Today you went to the 9 o'clock yoga class, what happened? You usually go to the 8 o'clock class no, got up late? The classic remains, 'What fish you bought today?'

It is great, as hopefully there can't be break-ins, but it can also be claustrophobic when you are used to the anonymity of the big city.

My resident Goan neighbours always greet me warmly. I think they love Haruki, our crazy lab, more than me. There is always a familiar nod, a smile and was there even in suspicious Covid times. Before we got here in June 2020, the newspaper, social media and grapevine were full of reports of how Goans had become even more militant and vigilant towards outsiders. Celebrities and movie stars with homes in Goa were publicly named and shamed as people were convinced they were 'importing Covid'. They were knocking on doors to check who was visiting or staying from 'outside'. I was warned of this so I was wary, but I felt reassured when I was welcomed back with a smile and a wave. Neighbours even dropped off fresh mangoes and veggies from their farms while we stayed home for our fourteen-day quarantine.

Those who bought, rented or moved here pre-pandemic have an air of entitlement as they look down on the recent Covid migrants. They suffer from the pushing-everyone-who-came-later-off-the-boat syndrome. They think, 'We were here first. Goa is ours.' Some who give me suspicious looks are wearing their ethnic cotton shirts and flip-flops with their adopted stray dogs and scooters. Meanwhile, others with their BMW SUV, Gucci sunglasses and Louis Vuitton handbags or their enviable dreadlocks and intricately tattooed arms riding a huge Enfield motorbike ask outright: 'You are a Covid migrant? Do you have another home in Bombay? When did you buy here?'

They complain about how the original vibe is changing. I try to say, 'The Goan vibe, you mean?' They are not sure. A yoga instructor explains, 'The village culture is moving from bohemian to commercial.' I often hear, 'I identify as a

Goan philosophically.' 'I have lived here for so many years and enjoy the freedom that the village allows me.' 'These newcomers are destroying Goa and it is losing its creative sensibility. They don't understand how the village dynamic works.'

I recently overheard someone in a Siolim store, 'We are renting this house. Isn't it so cool? The landlord lives in Dubai. They have a caretaker. You know how these Goans are, they all have these houses and property and caretakers since they don't live here. They are all so cute.' On the other side of the same shop, the conversation was not so kind. 'These Goans are all such useless, lazy drunks. Don't do any work. Just live off their property. Pick a fight with you for no reason.'

Many with second homes looking to buy a third come over to my home and complain, 'Land value has escalated over Covid. It is now three times more than what I paid five or six years ago. We bought three properties in Moira and two in Parra. Forget Assagao, it's gone crazy. The Goans are getting so greedy, asking for astronomical property prices now.' Or 'These Goans are so difficult to deal with. Calling us outsiders and shouting at us for not speaking Konkani. This is India; I can live wherever I want and they need to speak Hindi. It's the official language. Who do they think they are?' I never know whether to be offended or amused.

At the height of the Delta wave in April–May 2021, Goans pushed back, calling out all outsiders to stay away from Goa and not bring Covid, their aggression and their vulgar ways here. They were also calling out the cultural appropriation by many who claimed they identified as Goans because they lived here or owned homes. The dissent against outsiders was based on the belief that these 'others' were only taking from Goa and not giving back, and that they were indifferent to the fundamental issues challenging Goa's geographical heritage. This escalated when Covid was ravaging Goa with positivity rates around 50 per cent, which stretched the minimal health care system to breaking point. Too many people died. Goans went ballistic—they felt outsiders were bringing Covid to Goa.

These aggressions and microaggressions are played out on the streets every day. Goan drivers and those with the power of the language challenge you with hazardous overtaking, speeding and selfish parking. They park anywhere and will not move to give you a spot to park or to manoeuvre, blocking traffic. If you request them, they look at you condescendingly and say, 'You know I am a local, I can park anywhere. You go around.' The GA plates and the Konkani language are both used as weapons. You do not want to be in a position where you are overtaking, too close or worse still, gently touch a scooter—they will come at you in a lynch mob. Kunal and I know this from first-hand experience. The war is waged from both sides as often visitors have a dismissive, aggressive and belittling attitude towards Goans. With all the demands and shouting, the accidents and fights are mounting and creating a volcanic, violent Goa.

In June 2022, a video that was circulated with the title 'Tourists from Delhi' driving his hired Creta (a Hyundai SUV) rashly and self-indulgently on Vagator beach with the rising monsoon waves, went viral on social media.*

---

* Tiasa Bhowal, 'Internet Blasts Delhi Tourists for Driving Car through Goa's Vagator Beach. Video Goes Viral', *India Today*, 23 June 2022,

Predictably, it ended badly with the Creta pulled out to sea against the sharp rocks and Goans exploded. They named and shamed him, and called out the arrogance of people like him who are having a catastrophic effect on Goa and Goan culture, bringing with them their cancerous, consumptive ways.

Fighting Many Demons in Goa

I regularly read in the papers and receive WhatsApp messages about protests challenging the local panchayat, the state and the central government. Norma and Claude Alvares with the Goa Foundation and the Goenchi Mati movement have led the march against mining and environmental issues. Locally, they are hailed as our very own Mandelas.

Most recently, Goa has been fighting to save the Mhadei/Mandovi river so that south Goa's fresh water source is not dammed and diverted to Karnataka. Due to Goa's tiny size and population, its unique biodiversity and culture are overlooked when projects are planned on the national scale, endangering its fragile ecosystem. The other crucial protest is against the amendment to the Regional Plan 2021 that will allow agricultural land to be converted to settlement land, allowing high-rise and large projects to be constructed on huge tracts of land, further catalysing the destruction of Goa's biodiversity and expediting the climate crisis.

---

https://www.indiatoday.in/trending-news/story/internet-blasts-delhi-tourists-for-driving-car-through-goa-s-vagator-beach-video-goes-viral-1965825-2022-06-23.

Over the last couple of years, Goa has been relentlessly and aggressively fighting mining practices, the ruthless encroachment on mangroves and beaches, the heartless hacking of trees for road and home construction and the bad state of the roads.

During these tough times, residents have taken to the streets to save Mollem National Park and the Bhagwan Mahavir Wildlife Sanctuary at the southern tip of Goa, home to many species of bird and animal life including tiger from three colossal infra projects—the double tracking of the railway line, four-laning of the National Highway and the power transmission project. The other agitation is for the Goa government to declare all four sanctuaries in Goa—Mhadei, Bhagwan Mahavir, Netravalli and Cotigao—as tiger reserves within three months. The Goa Foundation moved the high court when a tigress and her three cubs were found dead (reportedly poisoned) in January 2020. In February, the *Guardian* published an article highlighting the concerns of environmentalists regarding the Goa government's denial of the presence of tigers and their ongoing deforestation efforts, which prioritize mass tourism and mining. This is in contrast to other states in India that are promoting tiger tourism. The article explained, 'The currently unprotected area of the Western Ghats in Goa forms a crucial part of the tiger corridor running from Maharashtra to Karnataka, which activists and the WWF have described as "the best and only hope for the continued survival of the tigers of India."'*

---

* Hannah Ellis-Petersen, '"No Tigers Here": Why Goa Is in Denial about Its Big Cat Population', *Guardian*, 29 October 2021, https://www. theguardian.com/environment/2020/feb/06/no-tigers-here-why-goa-india-is-in-denial-about-its-big-cat-population-aoe.

Despite the Covid-19 pandemic being front-page news at the time, this story caught international attention.

The judgment in favour of the Goa Foundation delivered at the end of July 2023 said:

> The tiger is a unique animal which plays a pivotal role in the health and diversity of an ecosystem. It is a top predator at the apex of the food chain. Therefore, the presence of tigers in the forest is an indicator of the well-being of the ecosystem. Protection of tigers in forests protects the habitats of several other species. Indirect benefits of preserving a tiger include several ecosystem services like protection of rivers and other water sources, prevention of soil erosion and improvement of ecological services like pollination, water table retention, etc. Conversely, the absence of this top predator indicates that its ecosystem is not sufficiently protected.*

In the south, civil society is fighting the Margao Outline Development plan that will cause the city and south Goa irreversible environmental damage. Lawyers and activists are litigating the monstrosity on the banks of the Mandovi in Old Goa at a UNESCO heritage-protected location.

In every village, residents are fighting to save their land and their trees. The Carmona village community in the south has been opposing a very large residential complex since 2015 on the grounds that the project would alter

---

* 'Declare MHADEI Wildlife Sanctuary as Tiger Reserve in 3 Months, Bombay HC Orders Goa Govt', Wire, 29 July 1993, https://thewire.in/law/declare-mhadei-wildlife-sanctuary-as-tiger-reserve-in-3-months-bombay-hc-tells-goa-govt.

the village's demography. Finally, in February 2023, this sustained agitation and legal action forced the big Mumbai-based builder to withdraw from the project.* Now, next door in Camurlim, residents are fighting to stop a huge development project in their peaceful village. In Pomburpa/ Ecoxim as well, the locals are litigating against another large luxury development project by a prominent designer. In October 2023, they put up a huge banner saying, 'Save our village, dear outsiders, no destruction of our hills.'

The Save Panjim initiative has been working to stop the construction of a pedestrian bridge and walking path as well as the ropeway project—a Reis Magos to Panaji cable car for tourists. Panjim, where the roads are collapsing even before they are completed, can't sustain any more construction and traffic.

In Siolim recently, there have been protests against the allegedly illegal road widening that has taken land from the fields without the required permissions or compensation to the landowners.

The other war happening is over historical cooperative fields popularly known as comunidade lands. By June 2022, the government was trying to take these lands away from cooperative shareholders and use them for 'public projects'. This is against the principles on which these cooperatives were formed and the palpable fear is that the government will sell the now priceless fields for 'development'.

---

* 'Finally, Raheja Backs out of Housing Project in Carmona', The Goan EveryDay, 20 February 2023, https://www.thegoan.net/goa-news/finally-raheja-backs-out-of-housing-project-in-carmona/95494.html.

I am often asked by enthusiastic golfers, 'Michelle, you are Goan. The focus here is on tourism. It is a major employer for locals. Why can't Goa have at least one decent eighteen-hole golf course? It will attract high-end tourists, not this mass tourism that is making such a mess. Golfers will even want to buy and invest in communities around the course.' I bite my tongue and try not to respond rudely since an environmentalist friend explained to me that 'Golf courses are an environmental hazard given the amount of water they consume. They completely erase local biodiversity as they need constant tending and weeding to keep the grass artificially smooth. There have been aggressive protests against golf resorts and golf communities ('Save Tiracol', which the Goa Foundation fought and won). More Goans would have lost their land and livelihoods, and it would have further destroyed the indigenous ecosystem.'

Activists are also advocating for human rights issues. With the huge tourist industry, serious societal threats like prostitution, paedophilia, children and women trafficking, child labour and abuse are being sensitively handled. There are NGOs, including Anyay Rahit Zindagi (ARZ), a social work organization, that is working to rescue and rehabilitate commercial sex workers, trafficked women and children, and find their livelihoods and homes.

Young people in Goa are grappling with unemployment, addiction (drugs, alcohol, gambling) and abuse. The historic influx of hippies and tourists, compounded with Covid isolation and over-dependence on social media have accelerated mental health challenges, depression and anxiety, creating complex societal issues of acceptance, medication, rehabilitation and hospitalization. A good friend confides about her son, 'What to do? How to help him? We spoke to the Father in our parish and he tried to talk to our Joshua but then again somehow, he gets those drugs. How many times can he go to the rehab place? He only must stop, no? Please pray for him.'

During the Covid lockdowns, like so many across the country and the world, families in Goa faced marital pressures. Due to the long history of migration, many men are away in the Gulf or on ships, leaving their wives and children at home, visiting only for a few days every few years. This long history of absentee fathers and husbands makes for a complex family dynamic. Mummy used to say, 'These boys have never lived in a family. They don't know how to treat their wives and children. Their fathers were not there for them.' The man's only responsibility is arriving laden with Christmas presents every few years—almost like a Santa Claus figure. Over the holiday, they spend money on shopping and partying, leaving the wife at the end of the month's holiday to fend for herself. These are resilient women who are managing jobs, children and money while riding scooters or driving cars. These families have not had to live through the everyday drudgery of married life. With Covid lockdowns, families were together at home for prolonged periods with no respite—relationships cracked and shattered. Alcoholism and domestic abuse grew into even bigger social evils and many never recovered from the financial and emotional stress of that time.

Interestingly, migrant labourers have been moving into Goa to work on construction sites and despite the difficulties, and lack of public transport and housing, they embrace the Goan life. Post-pandemic, I see growing numbers walking down my road to and from the construction sites every morning and evening. The men wear cargo shorts, shirts or T-shirts and backpacks with smartphones in their hands. The women wear their synthetic sarees and artificial jewellery. From around 8 a.m. onwards, they can be seen sitting at the main tinto outside the Siolim church to be recruited as daily labourers. '*Abhi Goa mein bahut construction ka kaam hai, humko Goa mein he rahna hai. Apke ghar mein ya garden mein kaam hai hum kar sakte hai. Please bata dena. Ek din key liye admi ko 800–900 rupiya hai or aurat ke liye 600–700* [Goa has a lot of construction going on right now, we want to live and work here only. If you want to hire someone for your house or garden, please tell us. Rs 800–900 per day for a man and Rs 600–700 for a woman].' The women have a far better work ethic and get paid less.

Over the course of the last two years, seven large construction sites have progressed within 500 metres of my home. The one that turned a knife in my heart was a sprawling, gorgeous old Goan house, a stone's throw from my gate with a huge balcao, thick laterite walls, Mangalore tiled roof and shell windows. I admired its grace every evening when I walked Haruki in the vaddo and now it's gone. The barricades are up and a huge project is being built at breakneck speed. The hurt was visceral and personal—I felt nauseous. Every time I see the big brown *patra** boarding up plots, I am triggered and start feeling emotionally vulnerable and physically ill.

With the new Mopa Airport in the north of Goa, thousands of trees were felled. Most concerning are the

---

* High corrugated tin sheets that are built around construction sites.

rumours that large tracts of land have been bought to build
a Vegas in Goa. You can land in Mopa, gamble and fly out.
Will the floating casinos and gambling move to Chapora?

There is a ravenous appetite to consume Goa. There
does not seem to be enough land to buy, sell, pimp and
plunder.

The Devil Is in the Details of Portuguese Property Law

Intrusive acquaintances ask me outright: 'How come you have inherited this house? We know everyone in the family inherits in Goa according to Portuguese law. How much did you have to pay them?' Well-meaning folks ask my sister Ingrid with concern, 'How come Michelle has got your ancestral house in Siolim? What about your share?'

Inheritance in Goa follows what's popularly known as Portuguese law. This is how most of Europe, not just Portugal, apparently handles property inheritance and succession. The law follows the Portuguese Civil Code of 1887 based on the European Legal System—the Napoleonic Code—where sons and daughters inherit equally. Good news for gender equality! However, historically, girls often did not inherit the house or the land. They were given jewellery and cash for their 'dowry' and asked to sign away their share to the brother/s. Now that is slowly changing.

Here is my very basic introduction to Portuguese property law—if your name is on the land records and

A photo of this house taken in 1966

you are married, then you and your spouse own the land equally. When one of you dies, your children each get half of the deceased parent's share. If there is more than one child, the property gets divided equally among them. If the children are married, their spouses automatically inherit half of their share and are added to the list of inheritors. This means that if one spouse dies, you cannot sell the ancestral property without getting your children's permission. These days, couples sign a prenuptial agreement that precludes the spouse from inheriting ancestral property if the marriage does not work out.

I will use my own small family as an example. I have only one older sister, Ingrid. When my father, Albert, died, my mother, Biddy, retained half her share, and my sister Ingrid and I along with our husbands then owned an eighth each. When my mother died, according to the law, the property came to my sister Ingrid and me. Since both of us were married, it was inherited equally by Ingrid, Brian, Bharat and me. My sister, Ingrid, did not want to live in

Goa—she loved her Pune life and the large, warm home that she and Brian had built on a plot of land inherited from our parents. My father had left me his ancestral home in Siolim. Even though my father's will was made in Pune, for the transference of ancestral property in Goa, we still had to go through a long-drawn process.

Ingrid was so excited that I wanted to restore and extend our ancestral home that she and Brian readily signed their share over (renounced/relinquished is the term) to me, which allowed me to inherit the entire property. We are a small family and I was lucky. In my generation, we have just two or three offspring per family, but these properties go back generations. Since they were all good practising Catholics, they had many children.

In most cases, the land records are in the name of a forefather—almost always male—and the descendants have not transferred the property into their generation. A Facebook friend who lives in Atlanta, Alice explains, 'We are from Aldona. We have a huge ancestral house and lots of land, but no one is left there now. My last aunt who lived there died some twenty years ago, so the house is falling down. We are around 80–100 heirs scattered across the world and none of us have the time or inclination to deal with the paperwork.'

There are plenty of anomalies that make inheritance in Goa unwieldy, including multiple marriages (in the case of my grandparents' and great grandparents' generation because of death, often of the mother; in my generation due to divorce) so too many steps and exes (not a happy situation), single aunts or uncles, those who became nuns and priests, adoption, illegitimacy.

Property papers in Goa were in Portuguese. Over the years they sometimes get lost, left in a cupboard as families move around, eaten by white ants or accidentally burnt when lamps and candles toppled over. In a few cases, families do have papers that are a few generations old, so they need to start building a family tree. The first step is to track down all the descendants of the person whose name is on the land records across the country and the world. Often, people may not be cooperative as they do not want to share their personal information over the phone or the internet in these frightening times of identity leaks, fraud and land grabs.

Then you must hire an excellent local lawyer to put all the paperwork together. In addition, this process requires regular visits to translators, surveyors, courts, *mamlatdars*, the panchayat, town and country planning offices, and the archives to get your property documents straight—all seemingly soul-destroying offices with painful bureaucracy. You have to fill in form after form, notarize, stamp and sign.

An old family friend, Aunty Melanie says, 'We don't have the money or the patience to go through the transfer at this age. Let it be. Whoever wants it, can sort it out. We want to just die in peace here.' As more generations pass, it gets worse. There are enough heart-wrenching stories of people spending their lifetimes sorting out the paperwork, where the stress of dealing with the warring factions of family and lawyers may have killed them. I know many who have succumbed to a heart attack or drunk themselves to death.

The laws are so intricate that even the so-called well-educated and informed people pull their hair out. You need time, patience and perseverance to get it transferred to your name. Many don't bother or when they do, it may already be too late—their or their ancestors' names are no longer on the land records.

Let me briefly explain the never-ending legal process of transferring ancestral property in Goa from my own experience and understanding. It begins with the inventory, which is the list of all the potential heirs of the person whose name is on the land records. Then the birth, marriage and death certificates of the heirs on that family tree need to be collected to establish their relationship with the landowner to determine what percentage of the property they stand to inherit from that ancestor. A Google sheet helps to keep track of all these facts and figures and is always my go-to.

Church records bring further complications. Since the Portuguese Civil Code of 1867 is enforced here, you need civil records and they all need to be notarized. If you are not a resident of India, this includes a visit to your embassy or consulate. Most of them were not operating during Covid-19. You may also need your Overseas Citizen of India (OCI) cards and a PAN card for proof of identity. Another bureaucratic, complicated procedure is done at the embassy/consulate in the city/country where you live. There, the affidavits and legal documents need to be notarized.

You need to make sure that all the names match on your paperwork as there are often different combinations of names—these could be full names with middle names (among Goan Catholics, double and triple barrel names are given with many convoluted additions to ensure you are blessed by ancestors and saints. For example, Antonio Diego Caetano Luis Carlos Edwardo Pedro de Costa de Braganza), both parents' original surnames, married names, middle names with father's and or husband's names (never mother or wife's names), official names on school certificates, marriage certificates, and passports. This name alignment requires more paperwork and signed affidavits— you will need to put together a name divergence certificate to solemnly swear that all the names with different iterations and spellings are the same person.

After establishing the heirs of the person whose name is currently on the land records, the next step is preparing the list of assets—the list of properties (immovable assets) with their survey numbers that these heirs will inherit. In many cases, my own family included, those lists may not match. A cousin, Clare, explains, 'My Grandpa's will and paperwork show that he owned thirteen pieces of land at the time of his death. When I looked up the current land records and I&XIV forms online, there were ten and the three others now had a long list of other owners with houses on that land with no mention of his name. The land records had been altered, the land was encroached and/or grabbed over the years without us being aware of how, when and where this was happening. As none of his heirs lived in Goa, our family lost a couple of his plots over the years.'

The next step of the inventory process includes legal notices about the intent to transfer the ancestral property to the current generation with the specific survey numbers. These notices need to be mailed to each inheritor to check if they have any objections and to establish that there are no other heirs or that the land has not already been bought or sold. This step is fraught with difficulties as notices are published in local papers. A friend in Mumbai, Milind, says, 'How are we to see these notices? None of us live in Goa.

How can we object in time? We have lost the right to our own property.'

Another term you will hear is the deed of partition (*escritura de partilha*). It comes into play after the inventory, in case a larger plot/s of land needs to be further divided between heirs and they need to figure out the proportion each one gets.

In some cases, there are multiple heirs all wanting to inherit the property, which leads to a secret auction within the family. The highest bidder gets to keep the property after paying the other inheritors their share. A cousin who recently went through it explains, 'First we found a surveyor to value the property. Then each of us put in bids for the value of the total property. This is a sealed bid. My grandfather had fourteen pieces of land and one of them had the house. My brother, cousins and I all bid secretly and had to put separate bids on each of Grandpa's properties. I won because my bid was the highest and had to deposit the money within five days to secure it. Then they split the money between the other claimants as per their share. My cousins were not at all happy that I outbid them and now won't talk to me.' As you can imagine, property conflicts can sour relationships.

I met older folk who are living alone and have no children or anyone to take care of them. They will their home to a niece/nephew or grandniece/grandnephew. An old family friend, Aunty Mary, explained to me a few years ago, 'It is so nice my niece Anita has come from Dubai. I have given her my house. She and her husband, Ivan, will look after me. I am getting old now, can't manage on my own here. I have registered my will and done all the paperwork as well.'

Some years later, I got a call from the same aunty Mary, 'Do come and see me sometimes no, my girl, I am close by to you at this home for the aged in Siolim. So lonely.' Then I get a call from Anita and Ivan, 'We are restoring Aunty Mary's house. We heard you also restored your old house; who was your architect?'

Goa also has its big *bhatkars*, the landed gentry who live off the land—not very different from the Granthams of *Downton Abbey*. Their estates are so large that managing their properties is their principal occupation and source of livelihood, enabling them to maintain their lifestyle by renting and selling bits of their vast landholdings over the years. When you meet them, they say, 'Just met with those Hilton people, they will be putting up a new resort in Vagator on our land. We are redoing the roof in our house in Assagao and will lease it to one of those Isprava or similar high-end property rentals.' They also rent out various properties to shops, restaurants, residences or hotels.

One popular solution for families with heirs scattered all over the world who have no interest in their ancestral property is to hand it over to a developer who then helps them sort out the paperwork for suitable compensation in cash or real estate. An old friend, Mario, says, 'They pulled down our old ancestral house in Porvorim and built a big complex with a swimming pool. All the boys in our family got flats. So nice to have this connection to Goa and our grandparents.'

Across the world, many families are torn- apart by property. The patriarchal narrative of 'only sons should inherit' is played out to different degrees. We know a property is valuable from the sheer rupee (dollar, euro, pound) value but it is more precious and priceless from the intangible—the sentiments attached to it. Everyone has saudade for the house their father built, their mother grew up in or they spent every summer in. Whether you are a migrant to another city or another country, you always want to go back to some house that means home to you. But once the grandparents and parents are gone, it's very tough to fairly divide the house. Many fall apart—the houses and the families.

In Siolim and across Goa in general, some of the Goan diaspora have left their homes and properties to charities with the intent that they be used to home the needy, ailing and destitute. An acquaintance I met in London, Judith, says, 'My great grandparents left Goa and then our family migrated to the UK. Since we are never going back, we donated our house in Siolim to an orphanage.' Though it is a thoughtful and noble gesture, the transfer of these properties is complicated and requires a lot of paperwork—I have seen a couple of convents in Siolim, where decades later the nuns are still struggling to get the paperwork completed to transfer the property to the convents' names.

If there is a legal will signed and registered in Goa, it can, in theory, override this bewildering property law. However, unless you are living in Goa full-time and are very organized, this rarely happens. Legal wills made in other states in India and other countries don't always work in transferring ancestral property in Goa either. Often, registered wills are challenged in court by disgruntled family members, which can cause further delays and financial hardship for those who need the money from the sale of property.

In May 2022, newspapers reported on the sheer horror of land grabs around north Goa. Unscrupulous elements in cahoots with powerful people were able to get the land transferred to their names with forged records and signatures. Dead people seemed to be able to sign legal documents and have children. It is truly terrifying how fast Goa is being bought and sold. The villages that were targeted were Assagao, Anjuna, Aldona, Siolim and Porvorim.*

Goans who choose to retire in Goa often prefer to live in the greater Panjim area. A city life in Goa with all the conveniences as well as the culture. A woman I recently met here, Sunita, says, 'We are so happy to finally come home to live in Goa. We know we are lucky to still have an ancestral house in the village, but we can't live there—too rural and remote. We visit over weekends, holidays, feasts, weddings and funerals and in May for the pre-monsoon roof preparation.' My friend Lorraine asks, 'What is the point of living in Goa if you live in a flat? Might as well live in Bombay. At least things move fast there. If you live in Goa, you must live in a house in a village. That's the charm.'

There are many returning Goans who prefer to buy their own flats and live peacefully in Goa. While some never owned property, others did not want to go through the painful process. Beena, a woman who recently moved

---

* Asmita Polji, 'It Doesn't Matter If You Are Dead or Alive: Your Goa Land Is Being Sold Under Your Nose', *OHeraldo*, 28 May 2022, https://www.heraldgoa.in/Goa/It-doesn%E2%80%99t-matter-if-you-are-dead-or-alive-Your-Goa-land-is-being-sold-under-your-nose/189987.

here, explains, 'We don't want to waste time and money sorting through the paperwork. We just want to retire here. At this stage of our lives, we want to enjoy Goa. We bought a small flat close to the beach in a gated community, very modern and convenient. We can't manage those old houses and village life as we have always lived in big cities.' They also advise me to do the same. 'Just buy a flat, easy to handle and clean. You can lock it up whenever you travel. Why do you want to bother with all the hassle of a big house? Dogs and gardens tie you down. Just enjoy life now, declutter and downsize.'

When you buy rather than inherit flats, houses and property, these transactions do not follow Portuguese ancestral property law—making it much easier to sell the properties.

Popular Terms and Types of Property in Goa

Some more types of land you will hear and read about in Goa are an orchard, agricultural, settlement, coastal regulation zone (CRZ), etc. All these categories require different permissions and allow you to build on only up to a certain percentage of the total land parcel.

A few more terms to make a note of in connection with property law in Goa are mutation, conversion (from agricultural land) or *sanad* and, of course, the all-important I & IV form, which shows the present and earlier owners/landlords (bhatkars) as well as the tenants (mundkars).

There is also a long history of mundkars on these properties—some families are grateful and want to give them some part of the house. In other cases, they may have squatted, grabbed, encroached and taken over the house and property, so landlords are bitter and just want them out. The fear of losing property is real, I am often told by family and neighbours, 'Why have you got that couple who work for you Aadhar and voter cards on your address? Don't you know they can try to claim your property?'

Happy Ending

I must add my own wonderful story here, as there is always a counterpoint. Good overcoming evil is always the dream. This is about my good neighbour Anthony Coelho. His mother, Natal Marie, was the caretaker of our house and property in Siolim in my grandfather and father's generation while they lived and worked in Poona. She also took care of my grandfather in Siolim when he lived here alone after retirement. Initially, Natal Marie and then later Anthony's wife, Maria, took care of our house and land for decades.

Over the years, Anthony worked in Kuwait while Maria (after Natal Marie's passing) lived here in our home in Siolim, taking care of this property and her three capable girls Marilyn, Francisca and Melissa. Anthony always assured Daddy that he was saving money to buy land and build his own house in Siolim and providentially, he bought the plot right in front of us, where they gradually built their own home. When it was ready and they moved out in the mid-1990s, it was both a blessing and a burden for Daddy as

Casa Mendonça in full bloom

he was older and had his hands full taking care of Mummy, who by then had severe Alzheimer's. But Daddy had gotten his house back because of an angel called Anthony. He continued to be a guardian angel for me as he retired from Kuwait and came back to live next door in 2008, around the time that our house extension was being completed. Anthony helped me right here, with lots of advice on managing this house and property that he had grown up caring for, telling me many charming stories about Grandpa. Amidst all this horror and hate of property inheritance and land grabbing in contemporary Goa, I believe that there are also good stories similar to mine.

I guess some things are meant to be. Some believe: 'It's God's will', others predict it was written in my stars like some sort of cosmic plan. It has shocked most of my friends and family at how an anglicized, spoilt, city slicker has become a Niz Goenkar.

And Then the North Was Sold and Assagao Became Gurgaon

My college bestie, Pritika, who lives in Chandigarh, called me sometime in 2022, 'I just met so many people at a wedding in Delhi and another in Chandigarh who have all bought houses in Goa. Should I be buying in Goa too? What are you not telling me? Where is this Assagao? Is it close to you? Everyone I meet is talking about buying in some place called Assagao.'

The quest to own Goa Dourado, our golden Goa, persists. Over the pandemic, every couple of weeks, we got calls from friends or colleagues wanting to buy. Most of the calls were from folks in Delhi, who were fed up with the pollution, politics, status of women, aggression and traffic on the streets, and felt that Goa was the perfect antidote—peaceful living, pure oxygen and a welcoming culture. Some calls went like this: 'Michelle, we are thinking of moving to Goa, which is the perfect place to live. You are Goan, you are living there now. What do you recommend?'

The two Goas

I had almost compiled a list of questions on Google Forms to ask: 'Do you want to live in the north or the south? In a village or a city? In a flat or a house? Do you want to buy or build? Close to the beach or far away from it?' And the single most important question—What's your budget?'

There were no simple answers. The middle ground we recommended was: 'Come and rent a place. Experience Goa and then decide what works for you. If you like it and want to live here permanently, buy it then. Each village and city has a unique charm. Some are similar, some are very different from each other. Some are still isolated and rural, and others are overcrowded and urban.'

We would get similar calls from NRI friends and family (typically those living in the Middle East and Singapore, some from Europe and North America) who did not want to face the brutal winters there and were looking to buy. They explained: 'You know us and our lifestyle. We hear Goa has great restaurants, vibrant music, beaches and an outdoor sports scene. Don't think we can live in a big Indian city anymore after so many years of living in Dubai [or Singapore], can't deal with all the pollution and the traffic. We prefer Goa. It has an international community. It's eclectic, has like-minded people, open spaces and a relaxed pace of life. What about medical care? Are there any decent hospitals there now? That is the most important thing we need as we are getting older.' They believe Goa is the right place to retire to. Again, our advice is 'Wait till you are ready to relocate. Come and live here, experience Goa, rent first and then buy. Maintenance is a hassle and expensive, and at the current rapid rate of development, you don't know if all the green will still be here by the time you retire. Don't buy it till you are ready to move.'

Luxury gated communities with sliding glass doors, manicured lawns and plunge pools are spreading like a rash all over the North. Assagao, Anjuna, Parra, and Siolim are the ones worst hit, leaving very few swaying coconut palms and paddy fields, the very pictures their luxury real estate brochures are selling.

When the state fails to provide the basics of water and electricity, you see why many prefer gated communities where they can Goa-proof their lives and keep out the trauma of everyday village living.

Over the years, after a luxe European car, a house in Goa defines your affluence in India. Many from Delhi, Mumbai, Bengaluru and Hyderabad now own second or third houses in Goa. I was often asked at cocktail parties (back in the pre-Covid days when you had to attend them. Thankfully, Covid has saved me from that ordeal). 'Where have you picked up a place in Goa? How much did it cost you? We are also looking, have been looking for a while now. Goa is our go-to holiday place. We need a house with a pool of course.'

The tragedy remains that a luxury lifestyle includes a mandatory swimming pool. They vary from postage stamp to Olympic size with many creative shapes and installations. These homes are often second or third homes used for two or three weeks in the entire year. However, the pool water and maintenance are year-round.

The difference between a Goan home and a 'these Delhi people's homes', was described to me by a neighbour here, 'We have balcaos, gardens and dogs. From the road, you can see people, plants and animals welcoming you. Our houses face the road to watch the world go by. They have high walls, big, locked gates, security guards and cameras.' He went on to challenge me, 'You don't want a pool, but you are like them—a lawn that takes so much water and a generator that is so loud and polluting.'

Then, there are those who go to great lengths to explain how they are not like 'those loud, entitled, arrogant Delhi people'. They have moved here to get away from them for the Goan way of life, complete with a paddy view and pool. They go on to give me their 'insider' intel on all things Goan, including feni and property. It leaves me wondering who the real insider is and who is an outsider/Delhi person. However, in their defence, the people buying in Goa are from across India—Hyderabad, Ahmedabad, Bengaluru, Chandigarh or Lucknow—but the term 'Dilliwallahs' has become a catch-all.

We try to dissuade people from buying a second or third home here, explaining the physical and emotional costs of managing it remotely. The monsoon is brutal, and houses and flats get mouldy if they are locked up. By then, all handymen have embraced falea* and it is extremely difficult to find skilled labour to fix problems. We always say, 'You come for a couple of weeks in a year, stay in any hotel. You can choose north or south. Try different locations each time. The hassle of managing a place here is crippling and not worth it for a short time. All your time will be spent sorting leaks, the electricity, Wi-Fi and inverter.' Their disbelieving look implies, 'You are managing a house here, how hard could it be?'

As property prices in some parts reached ridiculous highs, you hear rumours that a house in Goa now can cost more than a house in Lisbon. I met a friend in Mumbai who in 2021, chose to buy in Lisbon over Assagao. He explained, 'You can buy a golden visa for Portugal by investing in a house. Visa prices start at less than 3,00,000 euros, or you can purchase a house there for around 5,00,000 euros. It also gives you Portuguese permanent residence, leading to citizenship. So why waste your money in Goa? It is going down the road of all Indian cities with crowds, pollution and corruption. You can own a house in Portugal with the same or even less capital investment and get a passport eventually after taking a language test and going through some other formalities. We want to give it a try.'

On the other side of properties being sold, I also meet Goans who don't want to sell their house and/or property to non-Goans. John who lives in Divar said, 'I only want to sell to Goans. I don't mind if I get a little less, but I don't

---

* Konkani for tomorrow but roughly means 'Why do today what you can do tomorrow?'

want outsiders in our village. They come in and change the culture. Look at what's happening in the north. Look at Assagao.' Another friend, Wilma, also initially wanted to sell only to Goans, but she waited for years with no luck. She explained, 'Only one or two Goans said they were interested, but they offered me nowhere near what it was worth. None of my family is left here. My brothers, sisters and their children are settled all over the world. I came back from the UK to look after Mummy. Now I am also getting old. I need to go back there because there is free health care, facilities and concessions for seniors. You know buses are free for me. I am over sixty now. But it is so expensive to live there. I need the money for my old age. I can't earn there now. So, I sold it to someone who came from Delhi. They were willing to buy my house, the property, all the furniture, everything. They gave me a good price.'

Some days, I am weighed down by the generational responsibility of my ancestral land. It hangs like a millstone around my neck. I look at my feckless family and friends and envy their insincerity about their love for Goa. Happy to sell up, take the money and run. On other days, I feel proprietorial about the land and I want to savour and save it—the visceral emotion of belonging.

Over the years, Daddy was steadfast in his resolve, even though he never planned to live in Goa. He was sentimental and often said, 'I will never sell my Siolim house and property. I have inherited it.' This was in the 1970s and 1980s when most of his uncles, cousins, in-laws, neighbours and friends in Pune and Bombay were getting their paperwork together to transfer their property in Goa to their names to sell off or donate.

Pallavi, who is visiting from Singapore, dropped in with stars in her eyes, 'I have always dreamed of owning an old "Portuguese house" in Goa, restoring and renovating it. Coming here, this ancestral property law sounds crazy. I heard some strange stories that any descendant can claim they own the land and threaten you and file a case, so we have decided to buy in a gated community. Seems like a more sensible option.' She dropped in with her friend, Apurva, who was from Delhi but had been living in Goa since the pandemic. Apurva was unrelenting, 'We have done international deals across continents, so we have hired lawyers, realtors and private investigators. They have given us a list of properties that we are looking at buying. We have been renting here, so we know the locals and should be able to sort it all out and get a nice old "Portuguese house". We want to be in Assagao. All our friends from Delhi are here.'

A long-term resident recalls this modern-day history, 'Big-city people, predominantly from Delhi, started congregating in Assagao in the early 2000s. When their friends came to visit, they also loved the "Goan village life" so they also decided to buy. A few even moved here. As the trend gained momentum over the years, their Delhi restaurants, boutiques and builders all came here.' These last couple of pandemic years, the daily Instagram posts, reels, stories and YouTube shorts, along with architectural and travel magazines, all had pictures and articles on the Assagao life. More restaurants came. Some outposts from Bombay and Delhi. I heard rumours that the rates were climbing every week. Real estate marketing was labelling Assagao, the 'Beverly Hills of Goa', offering 'paddy view' and 'paddy touch' properties. Assagao—the village of flowers. Word on the street, however, was reporting that 'Assagao is gone. Headed the Candolim way. Everything is being built up there now.'

Other residents would complain that 'Assagao had become Punjabi Bagh', or Karol Bagh, depending on how mean they wanted to be. Delhi folks wanted to hang on to their pedigree and preferred to call Assagao, Jor Bagh or Maharani Bagh. Everyone else wanted to stay away. Friends from Bombay, Pune and Bangalore threatened, 'We can't live there anymore, we have to move out. Looking at Moira and Aldona or Chorão and Divar, no bridges there yet.' The original Goan families had long left Assagao. I ran into Cousin Julie who still lives there, 'We are a minority now in Assagao. No Goans left.'

Assagao has everything to offer—the joys of leafy, village living with the conveniences of trendy boutiques, world-class restaurants and all your friends within a stone's throw to visit and socialize with. The added advantages are the beaches and restaurants in Vagator and Anjuna next door. In Siolim, we catch some of the overflow with our proximity and access to the popular beaches of Morjim and Ashwem in the North. I recently heard, 'You know Siolim is now Bandra.' I said: 'Why Bandra? Because people from Bandra have moved to Siolim?' The reply was: 'Yes, that and movie stars. Those Bollywood types live in Bandra and are now also in Siolim.' I am still shocked that we were not the only ones here and unknowingly became part of some trend.

As I drive through Assagao, the charm of so many lavish, large and gorgeous old Goan houses with their balcaos, pillars, sentinels and gardens, remains. However, I am overwhelmed by the number of tree cutters, earth movers, cement mixers and water tankers I have to dodge, and the eyesore of the boarded-up plots with brown patra and huge signs for new gated communities—'Private property keep out', 'This property belongs to XXX', 'Not for sale. Keep out!', 'Luxury villas, coming soon. Call XXXX', 'Book now. Row houses with pools', 'Two- and three-bedroom apartments with views.' Plus, the number of chic boutiques selling fabulous and unaffordable leisure wear and home decor, expensive restaurants selling overpriced drinks and yoga schools offering nirvana, have sprung up.

Ahmed, a friend, recently dropped in to take possession of his idyllic villa in a gated community in Assagao. He ranted, 'They showed me paddy on one side and forests on the other. Now all I can see are similar glass gated communities on three sides and no water connection. Only bills for tanker water—no municipal or well water supply in the immediate to short term. How can they not give me any water supply? It's a basic requirement.' He was livid but had no recourse. Everything was built up and now being sold at three times the price. Vikram Doctor in his article in the *Economic Times* referred to them as 'villa chawls'— villas crowded together supposedly offering you a luxury experience, but you are so close to your neighbour (albeit with your own private pool) that it feels like you're living in a Mumbai chawl!*

---

* Vikram Doctor, 'View: How Villa-Chawls Are Reshaping Goa; Boost Tourist Economy', *Economic Times*, 3 December 2022, https://economictimes.indiatimes.com/news/india/view-how-villa-chawls-are-reshaping-goa-boosts-tourism-economy/articleshow/95947199.cms.

By the summer of 2023, the wells had dried up and water tanker delivery had also stopped in Assagao. There was no water but construction continued to boom and property prices catapulted.

Many sets of cousins from Mumbai who are all originally from Assagao would drop in and ask if this hype was true. They looked at me, bewildered, 'Really? Is the sleepy old Assagao now very fancy? I can't believe we are now going to eat in a fusion restaurant and shop in some boutique there.' Their families had all donated, sold or given their property away to extended family or mundkars, never planning to return to Goa.

East of Siolim, on the other side of NH 66, National Highway 17, is another construction hotspot. Mostly, creative folks (designers, photographers, filmmakers, writers) all live in the villages of Moira, Aldona, Corjuem, Nachinola, Olaulim and Uccasaim. A designer I met in Gurgaon, Mallika, mentioned, 'Almost my entire batch from the National Institute of Design [NID] is living there. I am still working in Gurgaon so I can't move there.' Every time I see a slick visual of another luxury villa community in these villages, I am overcome with saudade. Memories flood back of taking at least two buses to visit those villages— getting off the bus and then meandering down narrow, winding village roads through vast fields and serendipitous backwaters to reach their imposing laterite houses, that seemed so far and tucked away. I also smile as I think about Grandpa and his many jokes and stereotypes about people from Moira. Every time I share brochures of luxury gated communities and complexes with my brother-in-law Brian, who is originally from Nachinola, he laughs. He lived there while he completed high school next door in Moira and can't believe that it is getting so much attention. 'Nachinola? You sure? Can't be. Nothing ever happens there.' On the other hand, a former colleague, Charu, from Delhi will call saying, 'Nachinola is so quaint. I really enjoy living in such a pretty village. There is a large creative, liberal, like-minded community—I am renting there now and want to buy a place and move there. But the brokers are all telling me that Assagao is the place to be since I am from Delhi. But I can't find anything affordable in Assagao.' Moira has its own hopping restaurant and art gallery. Will it soon have more restaurants, shops and boutiques, and be able to take on Assagao? Only time will tell.

My friend, Meera, said, 'It took Covid to make me leave Mumbai. I am so grateful. I am renting in Moira. I moved with my driver, maid and dogs. I am never going back. I want to buy here. It is so peaceful and perfect. I have made friends with so many neighbours from all over the country and the world in our gated community, and all my friends from Mumbai are always coming to stay. Goa is the perfect place to live at this stage of my life. Amazing restaurants and awesome beaches. I can work and be on vacation right here.'

Serula's Salvador do Mundo is also attracting its fair share of covetous construction attention because of how bucolic and pristine it is as well as its proximity to Panjim and the Mandovi riverfront. The charismatic Saligao, Sangolda and their grand old houses are receiving similar interest.

Porvorim is an urban jungle—I call it Lokhandwala (a small suburb of tall residential buildings in Mumbai). It has a mall; huge electronics, shoe and clothes stores; beauty salons and restaurants, and is located between Mapusa and Panjim with good access to bus transport. Aunty Marjorie, who moved from Mumbai, says, 'It is so convenient living here. We are in Goa but have all our city conveniences here in our complex. Farmers Choice has everything for us. We have nice parks and gardens. The sprawling Defence Colony in Alto Porvorim houses beautiful bungalows in a well-planned community, which is built by officers who have served this country and chose to retire in Goa.'

Reis Magos, across the Mandovi from Panjim, has also seen a construction explosion over the years. The hill is being razed in the name of development and many villas, apartments and service apartment complexes with breathtaking views have mushroomed there. A millennial who moved here during the pandemic, Lina, says, 'We are renting this amazing service apartment. Very modern and well-equipped. Reis Magos is so centrally located that we can get to the restaurants in Panjim in like twenty minutes and on weekends, we go either to the north to Ashwem, Mandrem or Palolem, Patnem in the south and can get to either place in less than ninety minutes. We prefer going south, it's less crazy. We drive there for the weekend at least once a month in the season.'

During the pandemic, another friend, Aparna, who relocated from Delhi, dropped in. She waxed lyrical, 'Chorão is so rustic, I can rent a gorgeous, old home there for the price that I am paying to rent a poky one-bedroom in Candolim. It has a divine garden and a graceful tamarind tree hanging over the balcao. You can sit there and look at the river and watch the ferry come in. It is so remote and since I am working from home anyway, I thought it was perfect.'

Further across the Mandovi, in Tiswadi, are the picturesque islands of Chorão, and Divar. Their current attraction is that they are less accessible to tourists and make great places to live in peace and enjoy the tranquillity Goa is famous for. There is no bridge; you can only get there by ferry. The Salim Ali bird sanctuary is an added attraction for abundant bird life. My next-door neighbour in Pune and dear friend, Uncle Albert, is originally from Chorão. We grew up hearing him talk about how remote it was and how difficult it was to spend summer holidays there—inaccessible and cut off from civilization. Then again, 'When we drove from Pune in my Standard Herald in the 1970s, we truly struggled to manoeuvre it on and off the ferry with its low ground clearance. I really thought we would never make it back.' He always said the Chorão, horizon encompassed vast paddy fields and unending blue vistas of the Mandovi. 'When we were kids, we came for our summer holidays from Poona. These ferries of today are new advanced models compared to our good old *gazolims*. Gazolims were motorboats—they were overused and carried double the number of people they were supposed to carry. The result was that the motor invariably failed. I once had a nightmarish experience when our gazolim conked out as we entered into the rough water of the Mandovi and the boat sprang a leak. The boatmen used a tin pot to bail out the water. Fortunately, a fishing boat came alongside and towed us to the shore,' he said with a laugh.

After all these years, Bharat and I finally went to Chorão, for the first time as I wanted to see it for myself.

It was lovely getting there and back on the ferry. We drove around to find Uncle Albert Fernandes' ancestral land that was donated to the ñuns from the Fatima convent. I visited one of his old haunts—the cashew plantation on the hill with its view. I finally experienced the magic of Chorão. The other historic island on the Mandovi, Divar, is also remote and heavenly. Pristine and absolutely charming. I hear the residents are actively opposing the construction of the bridge as they don't want the development. Let's hope they can hold out.

Buying Up and Building

Anjum, Anjali, Angela and Anahita, all women of means with both time and money; the poder, Brian; Thomas, who sells mangoes; Prasad who sells veggies and Shezad who restores and sells antique furniture, are all hoping to cash in on this Goa property boom. Each of them asks me if I have land or a house to sell and to contact them first if I do. 'Everything is sold now in Siolim. Nothing left. Let me know if you have property anywhere in the north. There are so many buyers now.' The other evening around 5 p.m., just as I was closing my gate and going to walk Haruki, I was stopped by three men in a big SUV with a Delhi number plate. 'Are you selling? Do you own the land?' I felt like I was in some gangster movie being followed in my village. They threaten, bully and blackmail you to sell. They are cruising Siolim streets, stopping people and asking to buy their land. My dad's friend, Uncle Nasci, gave me his response to all these repeated requests to sell up with 'Ask my great grandfather. He bought the land. It's his. I can't sell it.'

I recently ran into an old friend from Delhi who mentioned she was in a consortium with other friends and they were collaboratively investing in restaurants in Goa. It explained the many restaurants in Goa that Goans claim are 'built by Dilliwallahs for Dilliwallahs'.

Another acquaintance from Mumbai who had bought in Goa some ten or twenty years ago told us about their insider real estate knowledge. With the help of their Rolodex, they were forming a syndicate of four or five friends to invest in property in Goa to develop and resell. They asked if we knew of any available in Siolim.

A Goan friend in real estate explained to me, 'The Goans sold long ago; now these sellers are all outsiders who had bought in the first boom some twenty years ago. They are now making a huge profit, many times over their initial investment.'

Joining the hot Goan property market are fashion designers and Bollywood wives—we keep seeing ads and social media posts touting restaurants and gated communities that they are designing and developing.

International giants Sotheby's are also in Goa looking at million-dollar/pound properties with clear titles.* They had full-page ads in the local papers looking to buy riverside properties in villages like Camurlim and Colvale. And soon after, a Sotheby's ad appeared in the newspapers selling luxury villas in Assagao!

---

* All the land records, 1&IV forms, historical and archival records are all checked and the property is legally in the name of the person selling the land.

It gets even more bizarre when some shady newspaper ads blatantly mention—'Disputed property? No problem. Call us. We will buy.'

Siolim has unravelled. It has some low-cost, soulless tenement housing with construction or farm labour sharing rooms and bathrooms. There are also flats, apartment blocks, simple one- and two-bedrooms like the ones you see in big cities—some a little fancier with a pool, some with pools, gym and landscaped grounds and some ground+one floor of concrete and glass and some modern with hi-tech controls. Others are palatial, with large courtyards, infinity pools and gardens (as if they are from Versailles) and have private jetties on the river to enter the residence. In old Goan homes with rich Mangalore tiled roofs, some of the roofs have the tiles replaced with tin sheets that are held together with a blue tarp, yellow nylon rope and a heartful of hope.

In the greater Panjim and Porvorim area, there are some townships with an explosion of buildings. They are fortresses with formidable gates, cameras and guards but there's no one in sight. People have bought a place for investment or as a second home and they remain deserted most of the year. Will this trend become worse or will they all fill up? The many who have moved, bought and invested in north Goa—are they here to stay or will the property boom collapse? Will there be empty houses, ghost villages and negative equity?

As you land in Mopa, the highway is lined with hoardings screaming at you to buy your dream second home in serene Goa. Who can resist that temptation?

Goa is paying an enormous price. The environmental toll has been astronomical as ancient hills and grand 100-year-old trees are being hacked down for luxury condos. In their place, are rows of frilly, ornamental, foxtails planted as landscaping. We can already feel the state getting hotter. Wells and the water table are running dry and sea levels are rising. In May 2021, we were hit by Cyclone Tauktae and lost a couple of trees. Our loss was minor compared to the devastation across this tiny state. Down our road, old mango trees, electricity poles, houses and roofs were casualties. Every monsoon wreaks similar devastation. Across the world, we are feeling the catastrophe of climate change—melting glaciers, rising water levels, wildfires, hurricanes, snowstorms and cyclones.

Joni Mitchell's iconic 'Big Yellow Taxi' lyrics ring true. We are 'paving paradise to put up a parking lot!'.

Juggling the Joys and Challenges of Managing a House in Goa

'So laidback here, nothing to do; how do you keep busy?', everyone who lives here is asked this question. The assumption is that you are either lying on a beach or in a hammock, eating seafood, listening to great live music, sipping a cocktail with a flower, an umbrella or both, and doing nothing—living the susegad life. All the popular culture Goa stereotypes rolled into one. Most of the calls I get are dripping with envy and go something like: 'Michelle, I'm sure you are relaxing in your pergola, reading your book, feni in hand?' 'I wish. I wish. If only!' is my reply.

Living here, you also need to be both a real estate and a travel agent—in addition to buying and renting houses in Goa, you are asked for hotel, homestay and AirBnB recommendations. I can't be either as managing my house, garden, fruit trees and dogs is a full-time job. It takes a lot of not just time and money, but also patience and perseverance—both skills and virtues I have had to learn on my quest to become a village Goan. When I moved here,

I needed to lose my big-city impatience and get used to the unhurried pace of village life.

Every morning I wake up with my carpe diem mantra, get into my warrior pose and wonder what surprise the day holds . . . 'Will I have to battle with the elements? Will it be fun, frustrating or will we be fighting for our lives?'

Let me account for how the months melted into years. When we got to Goa in June 2020, it was at the height of the fierce monsoon. The sky was always dark, hanging heavy with clouds and the fear of Covid. Our house was a bucket war zone. The roof was leaking. Monkeys had broken hundreds of tiles. Squirrels had made large nests. It was raining water and squirrels. It smelled musty, dank of wet dog, with muddy paw prints everywhere.

The time of the year to check on your roof for monsoon readiness is April–May. With the strict lockdown, we had not been able to fix the roof pre-monsoon and now needed to wait for the rains to stop and for the labour to return, to get started. We were not sure when this could happen.

Our three dogs needed to be vaccinated. The vet looked at us thinking, 'Who is this crazy woman who has driven here with three dogs together in one car?' A regular dog food delivery had to be organized. As markets were closed, we could not even buy fresh food to cook for them. Coconuts and mangoes had not been plucked. Appliances needed to be repaired and serviced.

We were also on high snake alert. Our friends Max, Gillian and Gabrielle, who magnanimously house-sat for us over the sudden and extended lockdown, found a baby python in the guest bedroom nightstand when they were packing up to leave in mid-June 2020. With rapid

Snake surprise

construction, snakes are being pushed out of their habitats, so spotting and catching a snake has become a routine village-life exercise. The standard operating procedure (SOP) is simple—eyeball the snake and try to identify it; if it is dangerous, call the snake catcher; wait for him to arrive and make sure the snake does not disappear into the thicket or the dogs don't get too close to investigate. The snake catcher arrives on his scooter, which could be hours after the call. He uses a stick with a big hook to wrangle the reptile and strategically shoves it into his bag. With agility, he uses his quick reflexes to close the bag while making sure the snake stays alive. He then takes it on his scooter to release it into a forest. You must save the snake at all costs—killing it is never an option. When big city folk visit us and see photos or hear about snakes, there is a lot of shrieking and exclaiming 'How can you live here? Aren't you afraid of snakes? What if you get bitten? Aren't they all poisonous? Why don't you just kill them?' Living the village life, you learn fast that you need to be wary of the cobra, the krait and the two vipers—Russell's and saw-scaled. The python can also swallow you and crush you to death, so you need to make sure small children and dogs are kept safe. Sometimes in the trees, there are bamboo pit vipers that swallow frogs, birds and small animals. The rest are all harmless. In fact, we welcome rat snakes as they take care

Catch me if you can: the monitor lizard scampered up the coconut tree to get away from the chasing Haruki

of the rat menace. On a routine vet visit, I met a dog on a drip bitten by a poisonous snake and I thought it was a pit bull. The vet said, 'No, its face has swollen up, it's an indie.' Fortunately, with the antidote and the vet's timely attention, the dog survived.

We became acquainted with our very own family of monitor lizards when Haruki managed to play with one of their babies. They are an endangered species, so we could be conservationists since we have given them a home and are nurturing these prehistoric-looking creatures. They are on our roof and in our garden. I routinely see Haruki haring off in hot pursuit and the monitor lizard scampering up a coconut tree, leaving a desolate Haruki on the ground barking his head off.

Goa Trivia

The monitor lizards also have a unique use in Goa. Their skin was used traditionally to cover the *ghumot*, the percussion instrument that looks like a covered mud pot. To preserve our music, making and playing the ghumot is being revived in Goa as a lively accompaniment to mandos. The monitor lizard skin has now been replaced by a modern, environmentally-sensitive material to allow the same sound quality.

Ghumot—a traditional Goan percussion instrument

Reptile skins have also surprised us. One morning, Kunal woke up to a perfect snakeskin under his mattress—when and how it got there remains one of life's mysteries. With our amateur eyes, we could not identify which snake had chosen to moult under his mattress, we just hoped that it wasn't poisonous or that Kunal was born under a favourable star.

Have you ever seen crotons in the rain?

'With plenty of water and nitrogen in the air, the monsoon is the best time to work in your garden as plants take root very easily' was some sound advice I got from a fellow gardening enthusiast. Pre-Covid, I did not love crotons, so my garden did not have any. These colourful, versatile and hardy plants make pretty village hedgerows and are very typical in Goan gardens. In this return-to-my-roots phase of life, I was determined to plant every croton that existed in Goa in my garden—I have had similar phases with coleus and begonias over the years and am now quite pleased with my assortment of both. Despite my deep love of plants, I have floundered with gardening over the last thirty years. The plants I buy often die while the ones I have stolen or been gifted, flourish (not sure if it's a myth or fact—you need to rob a plant for it to do well!). I went on a mission to acquire crotons for my garden and then found the right place to plant them—they are now thriving.

The list of chores to tackle every day is never-ending. Beyond dealing with plant and animal life, it extends to daily emergencies with collapsing walls and trees, sorting out overflowing flush and sewage tanks, managing water supply (malfunctioning pumps), plumbing and pest control (bed bugs, wasps and wood borers). Unfortunately, everything takes much longer to get done as here, time is flexible and moveable. People don't necessarily come when you require them or at a time convenient to you. They come when it suits them, at a time convenient for them and it could be an hour, hours or even days later than the agreed time. You must be prepared for delays and escalation of costs as the people supposed to help you don't feel bound to follow the schedule they committed to.

Additionally, as we know, phone networks are spotty in villages and making calls is impossible. You never know if handymen's phones will connect at all. Even if they do ring, there is no guarantee they will answer—too many variables, too much stress. All appointments are an approximation of time as there is always falea. You learn patience. You give up your strict rules of time and commercial commitment. You go with the flow. You learn to be grateful that someone has turned up to part you from your hard-earned money. They are not going to change so you need to get ready for the slow pace of life. At the risk of sounding like a cheesy motivational quote, if you get upset, the only stressed-out person is you, so it is best to stay calm and try deep breathing, yoga, meditation, feni or all of them.

Things will get done—just not at the schedule or pace you had hoped and budgeted for. This process has been frustrating for me in the past when I lived in another country and would fly in for a few days with a gruelling list of tasks to complete. Fighting jet lag, temperature changes and long delays were exhausting and expensive. Now that I live here, I am just grateful when someone turns up. If they are on time, it is a big bonus and guarantees them my business for life.

By the end of 2020, as things started opening up and labour was accessible, we started looking for help to put our house back in order. Miraculously, we found an electrician who managed to make our already dodgy electrical systems, further compromised by an ant infestation, to work. Smiling, masked and bespectacled, Kedar scootered over every other day, rewiring and installing something. Thanks to his wonders, we even have a working doorbell—quite a novelty in a village home. None of the many delivery people who visit us every day ever use it, but we do have it. Kedar loves our dogs and was happy to help with picking up our deliveries too. He soon became part of our household.

A loud and unwelcome invasion is the tribe of langurs who visit us every day. I accepted I was the real deal village resident when my concerns were focused on the monkey menace rather than the bigger global issues of hunger and hatred. Until I lived here, I thought of monkeys as cute, human-like animals. Darwin's theory of evolution proves we are closely related to them. Most humans have a healthy kinship with them as they are as clever and calculating as the best or the worst of us. You plant fruit trees, hoping you and your children will enjoy the fruit. In reality, the monkeys enjoy the chikoos, custard apples, tamarind and mangoes from the trees that my ancestors planted more than my children or me.

Once you live in a house in Goa, you realize that monkeys are truly devious monsters. They arrive in gangs with their huge families, destroy the tiles on the roof and torment my dogs. Every village resident has a horror story and an antidote to scare them away. A neighbour announces, 'The monkeys came today, jumped on my banana tree and destroyed it. Just light firecrackers. They get scared and won't come back.' After years of changing over 500 tiles a year, I reluctantly bought a few fireworks. Hearing the loud explosions, our three dogs trembled and went to hide under the beds. The langurs just looked at us and laughed. We felt horrible to be terrorizing our own dogs. Another neighbour offered a solution, 'Fill up transparent plastic bottles with some red liquid, the monkeys will get scared and stay away.' I was not sure if the red liquid was supposed to resemble blood or how it worked but I was not to reason why. We got some food colour, filled red water in bottles and put them on our roof. The day they were installed, I looked up, hoping they had run away in fear, and saw the black-faced langurs sitting on the roof next to the red liquid bottles, still laughing and mocking me. My self-confidence lay in shreds. They had won this round and all the others—they had won the war. To add fuel to my already burning rage, they came back in droves with their cousins and friends. Nowadays, they arrive anytime—morning, noon or night—and are a part of our community as a year-round phenomenon. Not seasonal.

Langurs on the roof mocking me

Every year, the rains bring around caterpillars, centipedes and millipedes as well as frogs and toads of every shape, colour and size. The frogs are so loud that you wonder if it is a dog or cat in distress. Some evenings, it's hard to hear yourself over the din. Divya has even named the resident frogs in her bathroom and our kitchen and doesn't let me shoo them out. She has a large menagerie of creepy crawlies in her outdoor bathroom to keep her company as if our resident dogs, squirrels, frogs, monkeys and monitor lizards were not enough. She may even have a pet bat! As the weather cooled down, we had a fabled visitor—a tortoise. She stayed with us for a night in November and left us early the next morning to hurry on to her next destination. Often at night, we are woken up by loud scurrying sounds on the roof and never know if it is field mice or monitor lizards.

From October onwards, our garden attracts a selection of spectacular migratory birds—living here has morphed me into a wannabe birder. I crowdsource their names by taking photographs or videos of the visiting birds and sending them on WhatsApp to avid birder friends. When they reply identifying them, I put them in a Google sheet listing their names and the dates I spotted them. We have so far, identified thirty-one unique bird types. These include varieties of sunbirds, flycatchers, woodpeckers, bulbuls, koels, kingfishers, warblers and munias. There is a chorus of chirping all day that I can't identify but I enjoy listening to. I was on a WhatsApp call with my bestie from California, Cynthia, who asked, 'Where are you now? In some Amazonian rainforest? So many different bird calls and all so loud I can barely hear you.'

My neighbours send photos of pairs of the migratory Malabar pied hornbills—impressive birds that they spot in and around Siolim in the season. We often encounter the big, black and beautiful low-flying great Indian coucal, Bhardwaj, in our bougainvillaea and frangipani. The month of January brings the Indian paradise flycatcher to our garden. They routinely make an appearance to take a dip in the lotus pond-turned-birdbath with the male showing off his long, elegant and colourful tail.

Extending, Repairing and Managing

In October 2020, we needed to start the work of extending the quarters for our house help here, Ajit and Reshma. They had a baby, Hazel, in January 2019 and we felt that the space they were living in was too small for their growing family. This meant finding a small contractor who was willing to build the room. In addition to Kedar, we had a couple more construction crew join our family. The project started at the end of October and I was promised that it would take three weeks to complete. It took six and dragged on through Diwali. At one point, I thought it would still be going on during Christmas. It was done by then thankfully. We had more construction crew join us over the year when we built a garden shed and a soak pit.

By now, it was December 2020. I had been looking for a roofer and was asking everyone I met—be it friends, family, neighbours or random people on the roads who I thought could help! I was told to wait till April, which was the right time to do the work and when the labour would also hopefully return. I tried to connect with the contractors my neighbours use. They often complain, 'These outsiders come in and throw money to get their work done. Now, these workers don't want to do our work and their rates are too expensive for us. We can't find coconut pluckers, tree cutters or labour to do our painting and roof work.'

Finally, just before Christmas, a school friend, Joni, who had recently sorted out her roof called to say that the roofer she had recommended was back in Goa. He had just returned from his village near Kolkata and was looking for work. We decided to get the job done and fix the roof right after Christmas. It turned out to be the right decision, as we later went back into lockdown in April 2021, making labour difficult to find between the construction boom and lockdown. What we did not anticipate was dramatic rains right after the new year. Our roof was wide open when the skies opened with thunder and lightning. Torrential rain poured right into our living room while we were having our dinner in the dining room.

By November 2020, coconuts needed to be plucked. It is a biannual ritual. This meant contacting the coconut plucker—a scarce resource and another profession that Goa and India are losing. Since we have only ten coconut trees, the process of climbing, breaking the coconuts and cleaning the trees is faster, easier and more economical for us compared to our friends and neighbours who have hundreds on their property. The coconut plucker arrives around 8.30 a.m. on his cycle with a gadget that attaches to the tree. The gadget has steps, using which he climbs up the tree with great skill, agility and efficiency. He is so proficient that to an onlooker, it seems like he's walking up the coconut tree.

My friend Sharon, who moved from Mumbai, was fed up and announced, 'It is easier to go to the market and buy coconuts when you need them. Who has time to call these climbers? They don't pick up. Then you wait at home for them. You gather all the coconuts and fronds. Sort them. Clean them. Sell them. Better not to bother with plucking

Harvesting coconuts

them.' Hearing this, her neighbour Veena, who has lived here all her life, rolled her eyes with a look that said, 'How can you not use the coconuts from your own trees?'

Trying to tick off another box on my own made-up 'Being Goan' list, we have found a way to use our coconuts meaningfully by making coconut oil. After the coconuts from our trees are broken, they are stored till they dry up. Then Ajit and Reshma clean, dice and sun-dry them. The shelling, cutting and drying take a few weeks before the copra is dry enough to extract oil. Once the coconuts are bone dry, we take them to the local mill to grind them into Michelle's Homemade coconut oil. Around 500 coconuts from my ten trees give about 40 litres of coconut oil, which we consume and share with family and friends. Not for sale, it has become a personal, home-made gift for Christmas, birthdays, anniversaries and to hostesses (better than a store-bought bottle of wine). A spoonful of coconut oil first thing in the morning is rumoured to hold Alzheimer's at bay. My dentist recently recommended massaging gums with coconut oil to improve their health and elasticity. Another Goan cure-all tonic beyond feni, we also use coconut oil and coconut flakes to make our homemade muesli. A brand extension of Michelle's homemade!

Michelle's Homemade

ORGANIC COCONUT OIL

(We're not sure how much is in the bottle, but we hope you'll enjoy this gift.)

MADE IN SIOLIM, GOA, INDIA

The coconuts are picked from the heritage trees in our garden.

We shell and dice them; then lovingly watch them dry in the sun.

Take the well-dried pieces to our village oil mill in the back of the car. Bring home the fresh coconut oil.

Let it stand for about a week for any suspended bits to sink to the bottom.

Then funnel the fresh aromatic oil into bottles.

NOT FOR SALE

This is the label designed by my friend, Ryan Menezes. Bharat sticks these labels on recycled bottles.

Keeping Haruki away from trying to eat the drying coconuts is a struggle—he loves coconuts and everything about them. He chews the fallen fronds, the shell, the husk and relishes the fruit, water, oil and baath (the Goan coconut cake). When a favourite person drops in, he will bring them a coconut as a token of his affection. As much as he loves me, if coconuts are being broken and cleaned, he's gone, hoping for some shell and fruit to chew—a true blue Goan dog.

By February, the tamarind on our tree ripens. That's when we need to shake it so the tamarind can be collected from underneath on a large sheet or tarp. Then all the collected tamarind needs to be carefully shelled and the seeds removed. It is then salted and dried and made into balls to store to be used for the rest of the year.

Thomas, the local mango authority, swings into action with his team during this time. They keep a keen eye on the mango flowers on our trees. Once the mangoes ripen, his crew comes over to pick them—a different tree each time. We have a few different mango trees, including Mancurad, Malgues, Xavier, Bishop and Hoot,* and they all need work and care. If there is a storm or a cyclone (like there was in May 2021), they need to be plucked in advance to salvage the crop. Thomas and team drop in to do their work at different times, each mango is hand-plucked and then let down the tree carefully in a basket. On the ground, they are collected in bigger baskets and sorted according to size and ripeness. There are many visits to each tree as the season progresses and each visit lasts three to four hours.

Over the Goan mango season from March to June, Thomas brings us a steady supply of the best of Goa's jewels

---

* Names of different Goan mangoes. Hoot means no name, when you don't know the pedigree.

A basket of freshly plucked mangoes from our trees

including Mancurad, Musorad, Malgues, Udgo, Fernandine, Xavier, and the Siolim's own—Manghilario. The sweetest you can dream of. Blessed with local bounty, we haven't bought mangoes now for the last few years.

In April, my garden is a riot of pink and blue with my bougainvillaea, frangipani beautiful, big, blue hydrangeas blooming. While the nights are filled with the heady fragrance of the night-blooming jasmine (*raat ki rani*), in the afternoons, the egrets use my lotus pond as their dipping and bathing pool.

In April and May, we also harvest the jambuls and chikoos. We had a delightful problem a while back—a family

Who is the reigning king of the road?

of bulbuls had nested in the basket of the contraption used
to take the fruit out (a long pole with a hook and basket)
and I had to sacrifice my chikoo crop so three baby bulbuls
could find their wings and fly.

Over the spring and summer, you are woken up to
the call of the koel, persistent and beseeching. It can get
annoying but is marginally better than the other village
crier, the peacock (I guess if you are so busy preening, you
can't also sing sweetly).

There are cows everywhere—on the main roads, on
the side roads, on the beach, at main Siolim's busy traffic
junctions and on narrow, critical streets. The black cows are
deadliest late at night as you can't see them at all. Mostly,

they are just sitting there or meandering down the roads, annoying you if you are riding a bicycle, scooter or driving a car. What is terrifying is when you see a herd hurtling at you. You wonder what all the panic is about until you see them running from a crazy, snapping dog.

One summer night on my drive home, I was face to face with the holy cows. I could not enter my own home as twenty or thirty cows were calmly squatting, camped outside my gate for the night. On the other side, my dogs were going crazy barking their heads off and running up and down.

Aside from the stray cows on the streets of Siolim and Goa, we have noticed big bulls on the beaches being walked (like a dog), bathed and groomed. When we wondered why these huge specimens were being given special treatment, we realized these were prized fighting bulls for dhirio.* Though the practice is now illegal in Goa, it flourishes in small pockets at the crack of dawn, under the radar.

May is the month when you need to clean the well as water levels are the lowest. The friendly neighbourhood well-cleaning guy drops in to remind you and on an agreed day, turns up with his crew. They pump out the water from the well with their own pump, scrub the bottom of the well and fish out any plants and turtles that shouldn't be there. Soon after, the clean well fills up with fresh water from the spring below.

In May, roadsides are full of street vendors hawking chillies, salted fish and colourful tarps as Goans get started on their roof restoration and the practice of *purumenth*,

---

* Konkani for bullfighting.

Making and stocking up on jams and pickles for the
monsoon (*purumenth*)

which includes the drying of coconuts, chillies, rice, sausages
and salt fish, and stocking up on home-made delicacies to
get ready for the long and brutal monsoon. You also need
to prep your house for the onslaught, so palm fronds are
plaited, gutters are cleaned, and plastic, tarp, and other
waterproofing precautions and preparations start gaining
momentum to batter down the hatches. It's so hot and
sweaty that the mangoes, jackfruit and, of course, urak help
to cool you down.

Our pomelo tree bore eighteen to twenty fruits in 2022
and 2023 and the Thai-influenced pomelo salad became a
staple at our dinner table. Most of my neighbours in Siolim
have their own fruit trees, so during the tropical summer,
someone will generously give us jackfruit, mango, passion
fruit, banana, jamun or some home-made delicacy. If you
live in the city, you look enviously at us village folk who
have the curse of plenty. But what does one do with three
jackfruits, hundreds of mangoes and dozens of bananas that
all ripen in this fierce May heat?

In May 2021, cyclone Tauktae hit us all. We had no electricity, cell phone or internet connectivity for over seventy-two hours. We were lucky enough to have a generator, so we were okay for the most part. But we lost a couple of trees—the fig tree that fell had to be cut up so it could be moved. We also had a jackfruit that had died the previous year and needed to be cut down. One neighbour, called me every month insisting, 'The branches from your mango tree are getting weak. You must cut them or they will fall on my roof.' Another neighbour also warned me every week, 'Look at your jambul tree—it has grown too high. You have to cut the branches. They will fall on the electricity wires and it will be a big problem for all of us on the road.'

The electricity had to be turned off for all this branch and tree trimming, which required all sorts of permissions and letters of application. It meant more government officials—the panchayat office, the forest and electricity departments—each of them bouncing us from one to the other. In addition to the forms and stamps, we heard, 'Electricity nah, bai. Falea yeh'* or 'Net not working now. Come tomorrow.' It should be no surprise then that these tasks string out for months here.

Neighbours Chris and Yves both told me, 'Jackfruit wood is strong and has a gorgeous grain. You can use the wood to make furniture, doors and roof rafters. It is lovely and will get better with age as the colour reddens.' I was excited but the operation was excruciating—getting permissions, finding transport and labour to carry the heavy

---

* Konkani for 'There is no electricity now, come tomorrow.'

jackfruit tree to the sawmill, and making sure they cut it into the required size planks. When I called the sawmill, no one answered their phones. Desperate, I drove over and tracked down the guy. He told me, 'Labour *gaon gaya. Agle hafte aake* check *karo.*' After too many calls and visits, just before the heavy monsoon set in, our son Kunal managed to get the jackfruit wood cut in July. Then the wood sat in my garage. A clueless city person like me knows nothing about wood and wood curing. I was nervous that this precious bark would rot. It also took up valuable space in our garage that was overflowing with village-life things—coconuts, pots, dog stuff, lawnmowers and gardening tools—leaving less space for cars, cycles and motorcycles. Just to add to my work and keep me out of trouble, I decided I needed to upgrade my existing kitchen. The centrepiece that emerged was an 8-foot-high, gorgeous, grained, jackfruit wood crockery cupboard. This took about six months of following up with various potential suppliers to design and install it. When Fatima (a migrant labourer from Karnataka who was helping me to weed and clean the garden) saw it, her reaction was priceless—'Madam, *itna acha* kitchen *hai. Aisa khabhi nahi dekha.* Picture *aur* TV *pe dekha, lekin aisa ghar mein kabhi nahin dekha. Bahut acha hai* madam [Madam, this kitchen is so nice, I have never seen one like this in real life in a house, only on TV and in the pictures. It is very nice]!'

As I continued to immerse myself in becoming a real Goan who lives off the land, I decided to grow my veggies. Truth be told, I cannot recognize leaves and plants by looking at them, nor am I someone who knows and remembers botanical names, what and where they need to be planted, or how much sun and water they need. After many hits and misses, we went to Yogita of Green Essentials for her professional expertise. She designed and implemented an elegant kitchen garden for us by the end of December 2022. Growing vegetables here is very risky, given how sandy the soil is and how an insect can eviscerate your carefully tended plants and dreams overnight if you are not spraying chemicals. As soon as we got our first harvest by the end of January 2023, we were delighted to collaborate with Sai of Posa who is committed to sustainability, local ingredients and community. She comes over to harvest and includes our herbs, greens and veggies in her creative, super-healthy salad subscription boxes. On Sunday mornings in early 2023, while Sai lovingly picks the veggies, I would get down in the dirt and go for the weeds (my Sunday morning ritual). I have finally been able to identify the different weeds and think of how best to get them out. Sai, with her commitment to mindful gastronomy and giving back to Goa, hosted a fundraiser for the Goa Foundation for Earth Day on 22 April 2023. She sourced local and seasonal produce including our veggies, greens and herbs for a fancy sit-down five-course meal—everything including the feni was fabulous.

I have had varying reactions to this endeavour. Some look at me in horror, 'Why would you waste this prime real estate? You can put up a decent house and pool on this plot or even an apartment block and rent or sell it. Siolim is such a premium location now, even more so, with Mopa so close and all the beaches in the north.' On the flip side, all my Goan neighbours, friends and family say, 'So good to know you are not selling. Let us know if we can help in any way,' or 'We must also try, we have so much land with sunshine.

Send me Yogita's number. I will call her to help us design an organic garden.' Another friend called to ask, 'Who helped you with the plumbing and the drip irrigation?'

I am in awe of all my neighbours and family who single-handedly manage their homes and gardens. They employ workers occasionally to help them with the garden cleaning and small construction work. They design, measure, buy the materials and supervise the workers themselves. Though, for me, it's been gruelling. I wonder how Goans are labelled 'good for nothing and lazy' when they lead such industrious, labour-intensive lives.

I used to believe that by taking care of babies and puppies, I had learnt all the crisis management skills I needed to survive in the big, bad world, till I had to manage a house in Goa. It is a living, breathing being with its own destiny that one has to nurture and feed. The action is non-stop. One graceful evening, I got locked in my bathroom. I had showered and dressed up before heading out for a nice dinner. Friends were visiting and were waiting to leave but when I tried to open the door to get out, it wouldn't budge. One lever had gotten jammed and the key would not turn. I spent twenty long minutes coaxing, cajoling and wrangling the door, but it would not oblige. Finally, Kunal had to scale up the bathroom wall and crawl into the window from the outside. He then helped me onto a ladder to climb out of our 7-foot-high window in my short party dress.

I realized why new luxury villas across the north offer not just rent back but also concierge services. Your villa comes with cleaning, cooking and maintenance services. High-end ones even offer restaurant, cruise and party reservations. You can avail of these conveniences when you visit and 'make bank' on the rental when you are away—an easy way to enjoy the 'charming Goan village life' in your own modern home without the everyday hassle of managing a second home—no Rapunzel wall scaling expertise required.

So having a house in Goa is not as magical or aspirational as it's made out to be . . . and being the *patrao** and/or the bhatkar is not as susegad as the stereotype suggests. I know, I know, these are not real problems but self-indulgent and self-inflicted and should be dismissed as #FirstWorldProblems.

---

* Konkani for boss.

Evangelizing Feni—Goa's
Exclusive Elixir

I went through most of my adult life with a healthy distaste for feni. It is an acquired taste—you either love or hate it, nothing in between. It has an overpowering flavour and pungent smell. 'I can't stand this. It is awful. How can you drink it?' is something one may hear from faint-hearted outsiders. I felt the same till I turned fifty.

A new decade, which was a definitive sign of old age, brought some serious tummy troubles. I know, too much information (TMI), so I won't elaborate. But when I came to Goa and the news got out, I was immediately prescribed feni. At this point, I was willing to try anything. When I was offered the Goan elixir for all, I smelled it sceptically—not-so-pleasant memories came flooding back from my youth, having tried and dismissed it for both taste and smell. But now, I was desperate. When I tried it again this time around, I loved it and there has been no looking back ever since. I was immediately converted from a sceptic to an evangelist. It is now my favourite drink with a pinch of salt, lots of lime

juice and ice. Finally, a true Goan! I now look down my
nose with disdain at lesser mortals who do not understand
and appreciate the fine notes of feni—I have acquired my
Goan swag.

Working at becoming a feni evangelist

I can confirm with good authority that feni is a spirit
only for the sophisticated—so pure that it leaves you with
no hangover. An uncle elaborates, 'It is a natural drink so
the next morning, you wake up with a clear head despite
any previous night's excesses.'

There are all the other lesser-bred, lowly alcohols like
whiskeys, scotches, malts, vodkas and rums and then there
is feni. Feni fixes it all. If you have diarrhoea? Drink feni. If
you are constipated? Drink feni. If you are running a high
fever or have a headache or any pain? Use a feni compress. If
you have a cut? Use feni. If you are celebrating? Drink feni.

Ulcers, toothaches, coughs, colds, arthritis, rheumatism, you name the ailment and feni can cure it.

When you walk through the hills in Goa in March and April, you will be intoxicated with the heady aroma of fresh cashew fruit. Friends will call to invite you: 'Let's go up the hill and find some *niro** to drink'.

Writing this chapter in March and April is serendipitous. It is the perfect time to write about urak and feni as it is their season. Since I was not suitably qualified and relatively inexperienced in this subject, I had to do a lot of research for the authenticity of this book. Every neighbour, friend, uncle, aunt or cousin claims they have the best supplier and theirs is the finest feni. 'You must taste it to believe for yourself.' I got a bottle from each one to test it out. I also visited traditional feni distilling stills aka *bhattis*† in Siolim, and sourced urak and feni from other villages and talukas, tasting and testing each to decide for myself which one I liked the most and why. As the samples kept pouring in, I began to embrace the spirit and enjoy myself, savouring the notes and the bouquets—I swirled, sniffed and sipped. I tried to sharpen my tastes to analyse all the hype so that I could hold my own with the best of the Goan uncles and aunties. Some fenis were just so smooth and others so raw— pure moonshine.

The excitement around cashew feni begins around December–January every year. We always check the cashew flowers in our neighbourhoods when we walk, run, cycle, drive past or visit anyone across the state, to make sure they

---

* Fresh cashew juice.
† Konkani for distillery.

are blooming abundantly and check the health of the crop. There is always trepidation and anticipation around this time. Everyone is invested as they hope and pray that this year's crop will be good so there is enough cashew fruit to make feni. The lockdowns over April 2020 and 2021, and the intense Omicron wave in January 2022, caused serious panic and desperation and predicted a dire year. How could we survive an entire year with no good feni during this already horrific, never-ending Covid pandemic?

As always, a little background—there are two types of feni: coconut and cashew. History suggests that feni was originally made from coconuts. The toddy sap was fermented to become liquor. Today, toddy tapping is a dying trade so we get very little of this coconut feni called *Maddel or Maddachim feni*. There are many popular Konkani songs still sung in praise of our original *maddachim* soro*. Siolim was famous for its coconut feni. After the Portuguese brought cashews to Goa, feni started being made by fermenting cashew juice. This cashew feni is now more widely available.

In case you are curious about how cashew feni is brewed, I can give you a quick overview. However, if you can, stop by a traditional feni distilling still when you are in Goa in March or April to see for yourself. I did it when I moved here and found it educational. It is only a 'small batch distillation', indigenous, family-owned business that works on demand and supply—they only make enough for their family and their regular customers.

---

* Coconut alcohol.

The cashew fruit can be yellowish orange or red

Only those who own the cashew trees and the land or are licensed are allowed to distil the feni there. Traditionally, one family owns the still and the whole family works together on the operation from collecting the fruit to distilling the urak and feni. My cousin William patiently explains: 'Cashew apples are collected from the hillside or the neighbouring plantation/orchards. The fruit must be completely ripe. Only the ones that have ripened on the tree and fallen on the ground are picked up with a stick that has a sharp needle at the end and collected in a bucket. The bucket was originally metal, but now it is plastic. The precious seeds are removed and sold off to be roasted for the popular Goan cashew nuts. The ripened fruit is then crushed in a sort of stone basin, usually carved out of a rock on the top or side of a hill. This basin is called a *collmi*.' It doesn't look hygienic and is gruelling work in sticky March and April.

You see families—men/women/children in their gumboots/wellies/mining boots stomping away (like people stomp grapes to make wine). After most of the juice is extracted, the remaining cashew fruit pulp is collected and tied into small round piles with some sort of rope or string. The fresh cashew juice is taken for fermenting into urak and feni.

The mound of tied-up cashew fruit is weighed down with a few big rocks and left overnight to extract every last drop of the precious juice. This juice is the niro. It is the last dregs of cashew juice that drips in the bowl after the bulk of the juice has been taken to the still. Sweet and tangy, it has roughage, which has many health benefits. During the season, every Goan family will offer you fresh niro to drink. Not water or lime juice but fresh cashew juice—it is divine.

The cashew juice is then strained to filter out any fruit remains and left to sit and ferment for two or three days in large (now plastic) vats. After a couple of days of fermentation, this fermented liquid is poured into a copper pot on a wood fire stove. With a pipe leading out of the top for the steam to escape, the copper pot is sealed tight with fine soil that is usually taken from a nearby ant, termite or snake hill, so that no oxygen gets in. The fire lit under this sealed copper pot is kept burning for approximately 8–10 hours till the fermented cashew juice vaporizes. William continues to explain, 'Local bamboo was used as a pipe before metal pipes came into existence. In traditional stills from the bamboo pipe, the condensation goes into a mud pot and they pour water on the pot to cool it. For metal pipes, the steam that escapes through the pipe then passes through a coil in a large drum of cold water to keep it cool and the liquid that drips out as a result is urak.' A limited amount of this urak is consumed and sold as per the local stills' specific requirements and orders. The rest is heated again in the same copper pot for another eight hours. The steam is again passed through a drum of cooled water and is liquefied to make feni. The alcohol percentages and size of bubbles are checked to make sure they are right. Feni masters don't need the alcometer to know the exact alcohol content as they can tell from the size of the bubbles. The alcohol percentage for feni is around 40–45 per cent and for urak is 25–30 per cent.

Since urak is extracted from the first press of the cashew fruit, it has a shorter shelf life. Available when the season starts in March, it tastes lighter, smoother and is drunk cold in the hot summer months. The feni supply usually begins around April. Since it goes through a longer fermentation and distillation process, it is more robust than urak.*

The secret of a good urak rests on its aroma, the notes it leaves on your tongue, the feeling, the joy and the scent of fresh cashew. You can dilute it with ice or water and flavour it with slit chilli, lime juice or Limca, or knock it back straight like a shot.

Over the summer, plastic and glass water bottles are recycled, filled with urak and stored in the fridge. Every year, there are a few mishaps in Goan homes when someone takes a giant swig of urak, assuming it is cold water and it always ends badly—with coughing, gasping, choking

---

* 'The Interesting Story behind Goa's Feni', *Times of India*, 1 February 2019, https://timesofindia.indiatimes.com/life-style/food-news/the-interesting-story-behind-goas-Feni/photostory/67788429.cms.

and wasting good urak. Feni stored in water bottles is mistakenly poured to dilute other alcohols, thus wasting good feni and creating a deadly cocktail of gin or whisky topped up with feni.

How you drink your feni/urak is also a test of how strong your roots are—Niz Goenkars patriotically drink their feni neat/straight up as they believe diluting it takes away from both the true flavour and their profound Goaness.

By June, with the beginning of the monsoon, the days start cooling down as it gets dark and overcast, and the time for urak is over and we start drinking feni. During the popular San Joao festival on 24 June every year, celebrations include jumping into a well to find a bottle of feni and then taking a large swig.

Every self-respecting feni-drinking Goan has their own secret source and supplier. The moment someone talks about his/her source, s/he is regarded with suspicion and immediately dismissed. 'He mustn't have good feni.' MI5, the FBI, RAW and the CBI have nothing on Goan uncles guarding their feni source. A cousin invited us over and as expected, offered us their own special feni. He assured us that his source was simply the best. It was. Since he loved us so much and was welcoming us to the Goan way of life, he was willing to share his supply with us. That's how Cousin Caesar called early one April morning and said, 'I am going to collect my 25 litres at 5.30 a.m. on Monday. Bring your own sealed jerry can and Rs 7500 in cash. I can pick you up near that bridge on the way to Morjim.' That Monday, we drove off on a secret expedition at the crack of dawn through the hills and beaches of Morjim to collect our treasure—Indiana Jones would have been envious.

The lady who brews the feni calls my cousin Caesar up in January every year to check how many bottles he needs. Accordingly, she totals up her demand and only makes just enough to fulfil it. With the cashew crop unreliable and her kids not interested in this hard labour, the supply she can offer is limited.

I must tell a feni story from when Bharat and I came to Goa on our honeymoon in April 1989. We were staying at the flat of our dear friend and colleague, now full-time artist, Neville, in Candolim. He had also generously loaned us his black Kinetic Honda, a rare pearl in 1989. So, there we were, romantically rushing around and exploring Goa on his scooter. Once, as we were navigating the roads of Candolim, out of nowhere, a pig came charging out and ran across the road. Bharat, with his advanced Pune scooter skills, managed to manoeuvre his way around and avoid the bolting pig. Before we could catch our breath to celebrate this narrow escape, out shot a dog in hot pursuit of the pig. It was too late to outmanoeuvre the dog—there was a screech, skid and thud, and we landed on the road. Thankfully, the dog got away unharmed and we survived with a few bruises—scraped hands and knees. Bharat had grazed his forearm while I landed on my butt with a bang. As we were getting up, dusting ourselves off and assessing the damage, the homeowners on that street came rushing out to help us. They immediately picked us up and used a bottle of feni to clean and sanitize the wound (yes, it works as an antiseptic too!). Even today, thirty-something years on, Goan hospitality remains unsurpassed. The resident Goan in every village is kind and caring.

The same day, when we met my cousin, William, he looked at Bharat's bandaged arm and immediately asked, 'Dog or pig?' Everyone in Goa who rides a two-wheeler knows if you see a pig, there is always a dog in hot pursuit—we just learned it the hard way.

William has, over the years, sourced the best feni in Goa and also mentored us in our journey to becoming connoisseurs. Serendipitously, William's family's ancestral house in Candolim was sold to Goan businessman Nandan Kudchadkar, who converted it into a feni museum called 'All about Alcohol'. It houses hundreds of antiques and artefacts including shot dispensers, mud pots and *garafaos*, some dating back to the 1500s. To understand and appreciate the distilling and drinking of feni, it is worth a visit.

A garafao of feni

My uncles have many fond memories of my dear Grandpa Jerry's feni infusions—they reminisced about how my Grandpa was an infusion influencer before Instagram. He used to cure feni with different spices and herbs and give them shots of flavoured feni to taste. William must have inherited his fine feni sensibilities from Grandpa. Maybe I did too.

Resident Goans prefer not to drink the feni that gets bottled, branded and sold in shops—they look at it dismissively and call it the feni 'for outsiders'. Despite my local biases, I must give a special shout-out here to Cazulo, a company whose bottle and label design is as elegant as the smooth feni inside. They package a range of fenis (coconut, cashew and dukhsheri) that are made the traditional way and offer an interesting floating feni-tasting experience where you sit at a table with your feet in a shallow pool. This is the same pond where they store some of their precious garafaos with their special feni collection. At the table, you savour this nectar, neat or in cocktails, pairing each with different fruits and foods.

By the middle of 2023, aesthetically branded and bottled fenis and feni infusions were all the rage. You could not enter a bar without someone hawking a fancy-flavoured feni. By then, I had owned my Goan Aunty badge and looked down at them with condescension. Thinking 'it isn't the real thing', I came home to sip on my very own secret unbranded feni.

Many Goans smuggle feni to all corners of the country and world with the belief that it needs to get its due respect on top of the global alcohol ladder. The Goa feni industry worked very hard to get the GI (geographical indications registry) tag* so that feni can only be made in Goa. Cashew feni is the first liquor in the country to obtain the 'heritage drink' status and got its GI certification in 2000.

Goan Trivia

Food, drink and agricultural produce with a geographical connection to Goa or made using traditional methods can be registered and protected as intellectual property.

There are currently a few Goan products that have achieved GI certification—the popular and traditional festive sweet kaddio boddio that we all love (also called Khaje), the spicy Khola and Harmal Chillies, the Myndoli Banana (Moira Banana), saat Xiranche Bhende (seven-sided okra), Agshi and Taleigao brinjal, Goan cashew fruit, the state's pride, the magnificent mancurad mangoes and the queen of Goan deserts, bebinca. Others awaiting certification include Manghilar (Siolim's own), Mussarat mangoes, dodol, urak, coconut feni, a few local rice varieties and typical dishes, Goa sausages, kunbi sarees, our Kaavi art, shell and coconut art.

As I continue to struggle with my own identity, I have discovered that a glass of feni helps with any crisis—Goan identity, Covid-19, whatever, cheers!

---

* The GI tag ensures that a particular food/drink is specific to only one geographical location, which supports local producers and sustains indigenous food and drinks. This tag encourages farmers to come together and grow heritage produce so that these products are not replicated and sold under their specific name anywhere else. The most popular example is champagne. If it is made anywhere else other than the small region in France, it is called prosecco, cava or sparkling wine.

Hoping to Be a Gin-Fluencer

It all started around my birthday at the end of January 2012 when two of my London besties Sczerina and Beth visited me in Delhi. They arrived with love and presents and were ready for an adventure. The very first evening, they asked me, 'Do you have any tonic or do we need to go out and get some?' I assured them that I did have plenty. When Sczerina pulled out a bottle of Bombay Sapphire, I was mortified— Gin was for old English ladies. I was neither. I was still in my forties and hadn't even accepted my middle age. She explained, 'Now that I am finally in India, I have to have a gin and tonic for the whole colonial experience.' I did not require further persuasion. Soon, I was sipping a refreshing Bombay Sapphire and Schweppes Indian tonic with a slice of lime.

It was love at first sip—the kind where I knew there was no looking back. This exclusive love affair with Bombay Sapphire continued till mid-2019 when my friend Biren, with his extensive knowledge and stocks of gin, organized an informal gin tasting for me at his home in Bengaluru complete with a clipboard to record the notes and the botanicals. It was a life-changing experience that expanded my horizons. There were so many tastes and tones—the juniper berries, the spices, the herbs—a world of gin that existed beyond Bombay Sapphire. I started eulogizing the alchemies and discussing the virtues of copper pot and London dry while tasting the notes of cinnamon, pepper, vanilla, orange and grapefruit, and the bouquets of blueberry, lavender and bergamot.

Gin has come a long way from its rotgut days and the gin industry has boomed around the world and closer home in Goa. Greater Than, Hapusa and Stranger & Sons were the original Goan gins that began this revolution in 2017. The global gin explosion is so big that the *New Yorker* did a detailed piece in December 2019 on this resurgence, using hard data to support its 'freakish phenomenon' tag and ridiculing the popular term 'ginnaissance'.* I have been doing my bit to support this noble cause beyond feni to reinforce the drunk village Goan stereotype and to break societal prejudices that claim it is not acceptable for women to drink. Both feni and gin are ideal for our warm tropical climate and go down well with a slice of lime.

Friends from around the world periodically share photos of their local favourites and we add them to the list of gins to taste. When we went to Japan and tried their Roku, I was not sure if I loved the bottle or its subtle sakura flavour more. In South Africa, I tasted a gin with pure gold flecks but

---

* Anthony Lane, 'The Intoxicating History of Gin', *New Yorker*, 2 December 2019, https://www.newyorker.com/magazine/2019/12/09/the-intoxicating-history-of-gin.

avoided the one made with elephant dung. In Stockholm, I went with my besties, Ragini and Tanu, to the acclaimed Hernö Gin Bar to pay homage to the world's leading and most awarded gin producer. Once the news was out that I loved gin beyond Bombay Sapphire, bottles of Bathtub (love the brown paper label and the light flavour), Sipsmith (very English), Botanist (too many botanicals for me but has an impressive bottle), Caorunn (struggled to pronounce it like the Scots but love the gin), the popular Tanqueray and Hendricks (not a fan of the strong cucumber taste) poured in from friends and family's duty-free shopping (pre-Covid). It all snowballed and I was swimming in gin by early 2020. I celebrated my birthday in January 2020 with my own do-it-yourself (DIY) mixology gin-tasting evening, where we offered a variety of infusions (cinnamon, orange, mint, chilli) and mixers (flavoured tonics, soda and juices) and a game that asked our guests to rate their favourite gin on a few parameters including taste, smell and botanicals. That's how I found myself in a great place to survive the liquor lockdown in Mumbai in March 2020. While we rationed my large gin supplies for the three-month lockdown, many friends who were struggling resorted to buying alcohol from the black market at exorbitant prices in Mumbai by May 2020.

In 2020, despite the pandemic, Goa saw the launch of a host of new gins—Tickle, Pumori, Clearly Good, Great Than Juniper bomb and Samsara. I am fascinated by Clearly Good's pint-sized bottle and its changing colour to blue when diluted, and Pumori's strong cardamom flavour. My current favourite is Samsara for its well-rounded appeal—perfect when mixed with tonic or muddled with oranges

Michelle's birthday gin celebration in January 2020

and topped with lots of crushed ice. I tasted and tried each of these for the greater good of helping family and friends to make the right choice. In 2021, more gin brands were born. There was Amrut Nilgiris (from Amrut Distilleries in Bengaluru), a lovely lightly flavoured gin, Seqer (a blue bottle with strong Goan roots), Jin Jinji (Darjeeling tea botanicals) and GinGin (reportedly made with hemp, it has a luscious taste and a slick bottle and logo). In 2022, there were Matinee (jazzy label), Tamras (tasteful label and bottle, also offers distillery tours and tastings), Doja (a marriage of Japanese and Indian sensibilities and spices), Satiwa (the temptation of the heady hemp), Terry Sent Me! (interesting name, bottle and gin) and many iterations and pinks of the OG Greater Than, Stranger & Sons and Samsara. Short

Story launched three white spirits—gin, vodka and rum—at the end of 2022. Their dry gin with the green label is gentle and wholesome with a citrus flavour. I have enjoyed it straight with ice with an infusion of orange and tonic.

Too many gins, too little time—most were produced, and test-marketed in Goa before they were sold in the major Indian metros. Since Goa has one of the lowest rates of alcohol taxation in India and a regular supply of tourists looking to party, plenty of gin distillers are setting up shop in Goa.* These gins end up costing a fraction of the price here when compared to other states across the country with higher alcohol excise duties. Goa is significantly cheaper than neighbouring Maharashtra and Karnataka—another reason to drink homegrown.

The original Schweppes Indian tonic remains my favourite. However, cashing in on this gin-explosion are a variety of new tonics including Svami, Fever Tree and Sepoy. Each of them comes in a range of colours, flavours and quantities of sugar. Some are riding the hard seltzers wave exploding in Goa and across the world—you can even grab a pre-mixed Bombay Sapphire and tonic or a Jack and Coke in a can along with many other flavoured gins and vodkas.

Talking about other popular liquors—Desmondji here is making some very good agave (tequila) and cachaça (cane rum). We have mixed marvellous margaritas and muddled caipirinhas regularly and reasonably with them. Mahua is

---

* Tina Das, 'Tulsi to Strawberry—How Desi Gin from Goa Is Converting India's Vodka Loyalists', Print, 10 September 2022, https://theprint.in/feature/tulsi-to-strawberry-how-desi-gin-from-goa-is-converting-indias-vodka-loyalists/1120453/.

another indigenous Indian liquor that has a unique flowery flavour and has gotten a good reception in the cool cocktail circuit. Another agave entrant is the beautifully packaged and bottled Pistola. It is smooth with a 'good old lick of salt and lime before downing the shot' routine.

I don't drink whisky and know very little about the growing trends of whiskies, scotches and single malts. But I have heard on good authority from discerning whisky drinkers across the world that Goa's very own Paul John has collected a large local, national and international following. Watch out Scotland, here comes Goa.

The college staple Old Monk has a couple of challengers in Goa—Makazai (translates to 'I want' in Konkani), Segredo Aldeia (its café version is smooth and exquisite, and only needs a cube of ice) and Earth (rustic spiced rum that is ethically packaged). I will never be able to give up Old Monk and I am sure it will always have a cult following, but the local coconut rum, Cabo, I hear, can take on Malibu.

Occasionally, on a hot Goan evening when I choose to drink beer, I find that there are always new beer brands available—IPAs, lagers, wheat beers and more to choose from. Initially, it was just Bira but Sleepy Owl, Susegado and Simba came in as well. The Goa Brewing Company has a few artisanal craft beers including wheat and pineapple flavours, Eight Finger Eddie and the rice beer, People's Lager. People's is brewed from an heirloom variety of rice with deep roots in Goan heritage, the company is committed to sourcing the rice and other ingredients from the village farmers. The bottle and the beer are cool too.

One final word of advice for amateur gin drinkers from me, the wannabe gin-fluencer—avoid all the variants, the bottled pre-mixes, pinks and infusions. Pull out your top-drawer gin and live your best mixologist life. If you want to stay classic— shake (never stir, obviously) your own dirty martinis with those olives, pour G&Ts and gimlets, make your very own pink gin or get adventurous and recreate your favourite cocktail at home. Ours is called Peru Meru— you need to mix guava juice, lime juice, ice, chilli and salt in a cocktail shaker and then pour it into a glass rimmed with chilli powder and salt (for that extra kick at the end). Depending on how I am feeling, I top it with either feni or gin.

Note: These two chapters on feni and gin have been written in a light-hearted, tongue-in-cheek vein. They are not to promote or encourage drinking. If you suffer from alcoholism or any other addiction, depression or any mental health illness, please do not drink. Don't drink and drive either.

Learning Goan Celebrations
and Traditions

In my quest to become an authentic village Goan, I am determined to understand and embrace the myriad traditions and festivals that are observed here. Each season and month brings a new celebration.

Over the years, I have attended neighbours' housewarmings, first communions, confirmations and *Saibinn** home visits. In September and October every year after Mother Mary's birthday on 8 September, a statue of her is taken from house to house to build community. When I'm walking Haruki, I see the statue being carried in a procession in the evenings to the homes of devout Catholics in the vaddo. I have heard the hymns and prayers in Konkani, admired the candles and flowers and relished a few snacks, the most delicious was always the boiled chana with bits of freshly sliced coconut. In 2022 and 2023, Ajit and Reshma's community adapted

---

* A tradition when Mary's statue is taken from house to house while specific prayers are recited, and hymns are sung.

this Goan Saibinn tradition and brought her from home to home, saying the prayers in Hindi.

At other times, when I walk Haruki in the evenings, I hear the sweet singing of hymns and the chorus of *ladinha**
prayers in front of the crosses that pepper our vaddo. Usually sung in May, they seem to be in many languages— Latin, Portuguese and Konkani (all Greek to me). There is harmonizing and it all sounds melodious and meditative. Sometimes you can also hear a violin or a guitar.

Neighbours Irene and Maria explain, 'There is a children's cross, *Burgian cho Khuris*, in our vaddo. The feast of this cross is celebrated in January after the Siolim church feast to *Nossa Senhora de Guia*.† There are nine days of *novena*‡ prayers and the tenth day is the feast. Around this children's cross in our vaddo, we also have community prayers every month, usually on the first Sunday. You must join us, Michelle, now that you live here.'

I love eating the sweet gingery kaddio boddio,§ sorpotel¶ and sannas** at every feast. Since we moved here, we have tried to make patoleo†† on 15 August every year for the feast of the Assumption (15 August is believed to be the day that Mary was assumed body and soul into heaven).

---

* Portuguese for litany. A litany is a series of prayers or invocations, typically to Our Lady or a particular saint.
† Portuguese for Our Lady of the Guide.
‡ A form of worship in the Roman Catholic church consisting of special prayers or services on nine successive days.
§ A Goan sweet of besan and jaggery flavoured with ginger made at feasts. It was recently GI-tagged.
¶ A spicy, vinegary, pork dish of Portuguese origin.
** Fermented toddy steamed rice cakes.
†† A sweet made with rice, jaggery and coconut batter steamed in turmeric leaves. It has a history in the indigenous harvest festival, also originally celebrated on 15 August.

The altar in our home is decorated to be blessed after
Easter in April 2021

One very important event on the calendar for all
practising Catholics is the blessing of the home after Easter.
The priest follows a tight schedule due to the number of
homes he has to bless across the parish. Hence, everyone
is allotted an exact date and time slot according to the
neighbourhood *samudai*.* As per the local church's SOP,
we tie up our dogs, stuff the envelope with cash, light the
candles and arrange the flowers in front of our old family
altar. Upon seeing me, the priest kindly obliges us with the
prayers in English. However, when he formally blessed the
house's new extension in December 2009, all the prayers
were in Konkani.

---

* Konkani for a small Christian community.

Our family altar has probably been in this house for the last 160 years of its existence and has been blessed most years. An altar remains an important part of any Goan Catholic home—blessings before leaving for a journey and before weddings are all done in front of the family altar. Older folk explain, 'Old houses had ivory and bone statues, often with gold or silver inlay that has since been broken into and robbed.' With all these houses coming down or being sold, we see many beautiful antique carved wooden altars for sale in shops that sell furniture along the roads. You can also see them as décor in homes and hotels across Goa without the religious sanctity.

Four Funerals and a Wedding

At my dear neighbour, Anthony's funeral, there was a brass band. Grandpa Jerry and my aunt, Sister Maryann (my dad's sister) are buried in the Siolim cemetery. The flower arrangements on the graves in Goa and at All Souls Day on 2 November can take on the Chelsea Flower Show. The big 'Aiz Maka, Falea Tuka' sign outside Siolim's and most village graveyards is both funny and sobering. Literally translated, it is 'today me, tomorrow you'—another reminder of how ephemeral life is. The Japanese have their cherry blossoms and we have our graveyards screaming 'Aiz Maka, Falea Tuka'.

With our preoccupation with peace in the afterlife, the one popular Goan hobby I can't bring myself to embrace is scouring the morning papers for the obituaries, anniversaries and month's minds (remembrance masses to pray for the departed souls after one month and one year). Today, obituaries are circulated more efficiently with WhatsApp and Facebook groups.

I attend funerals to honour a parent, aunt or dear friend, to pay last respects and for closure, in person or online. However, I have seen siblings and family members of the deceased not speaking to each other as they are at war over who someone married or ancestral property or are too busy with their diasporic lives. The nuns at the Siolim St Joseph's Home for the Aged often told me heartbreaking stories: 'When they are alive, they sit here on this balcony and wait every evening, hoping that someone will come to visit. Often, they wander off to the main road looking for their family. No one comes. But when they die, the relatives turn up to pay their last respects at the funeral and demand their possessions and bank accounts. It is so sad.' I know of an aunt who did not visit or speak to her sister for years because of some disagreement. But, as soon as her sister died, she made sure that the funeral arrangements were delayed so that she could cry bitterly as the chief mourner, inconsolable after the loss. Making sure the person's soul is at peace in the afterlife extends to elaborately decorating graves and flying in for birth and death anniversaries of the dear departed. My personal belief and something I try to live by, is to spend time with those you value when they are alive.

The other preoccupation with photographing, and during and after the pandemic, live streaming the open casket for everyone to see close-ups of the corpse are all too morbid for me. I can't stomach those visuals. I prefer to treasure photos of a happy, smiling, living, human being.

After four funerals, there is usually a wedding. Weddings have at least three or four days of celebrations. In Goa, you need to be civilly married first and have a registered marriage certificate before you can get married in a catholic church.

A day or two before the wedding is the *roce* when coconut milk is poured over the bride and groom. As with many Goan syncretic celebrations, the roce has roots in Catholicism, Hinduism and animism. A consolidation of many belief systems, it is done to wash away your sins, cleanse, welcome the couple to the carnal joys of marriage and bless them with children. Neighbours explain to me, 'It always starts with a prayer, a blessing and then we sing some *mandos*.' I have witnessed the roce bastardized beyond coconut milk to include breaking raw eggs on the heads of the captive bride and groom.

On the day of the wedding, just before the mass, the bride and groom are blessed by elders in the family in front of the altar at home. Altars are elaborately decorated for this tradition and photo op where beyond the parents and grandparents, the blessings extend to godparents, aunts, uncles, grandaunts and granduncles. The wedding mass is a solemn event where guests turn up in their modest, tailored, sequin dresses, and suits. There is a choir with an organ singing in perfect harmony. The bride dressed in her beautiful white dress walks down the aisle with her parents and an entourage of flower girls, pageboys, bridesmaids and groomsmen. The groom sweats it out in his tie and suit waiting with his best man at the church altar. My mother and both grandmothers wore white dresses, as did many cousins and friends. My sister, Ingrid and I chose to wear rich silk Banarasi sarees (maroon and magenta).

A Goan Catholic wedding reception is a rambunctious evening. When the bridal couple arrives, confetti is thrown to welcome them. It was originally rice (another symbol of fertility), then terrible thermocol, and now more eco-friendly flowers. There are traditional toasts raised by family, friends or prominent members of the community offering advice followed by a choreographed cutting of a three-tiered wedding cake with marzipan fondant icing. Guests are offered a shot-sized glass of sweet port wine and a slice of plum cake to toast the couple. Champagne is popped by the best man, but only the wedding party gets to drink the champagne while the rest of the guests just watch. There is live music, a band, (full, three-person or one-person) or DJ, and an MC who talks too much, often gives lame advice on marriage and cracks lamer chauvinistic jokes. The dance festivities start with a community bridal grand march to Mendelssohn's 'Wedding March', followed by lots of dancing, line dancing and frenetic jiving. The party really gets going to a medley of lively tunes called the *Goan masala,* which usually includes YMCA, Maria Pitache,* the birdy song,† the Macarena and Konkani favourites. There is flowing feni and a table heaving with traditional Goan delicacies. The reception ends with the bride throwing the bouquet for a single woman to catch (marking her as the next to get married) and the grand finale is when the bride and groom are carried on chairs by able-bodied folks to lots of drama, drum rolls and upbeat and suspenseful music for a kiss.

---

* A popular party favourite composed by Remo Fernandes. It is a Goan-based song but folk entertainment from Daman (another Portuguese colony) in the Portuguese. The song tells the tale of a girl named Maria, whose father promised the boy to give his daughter's hand in marriage, but cheated and gave Maria to a wealthier suitor.

† Chicken Dance.

Goans dismiss the trend of sangeets at Indian weddings (another Bollywood-influenced tradition). They feel that 'We have good fun, music, dancing and drinking at our receptions. What rubbish those sangeets are, some practised dances and some dress code and all. Telling you what colour to wear and then sitting down and watching all those people dance on some stage. Everyone dances so well at all our Goan weddings no, without those rehearsals and choreographers.'

The day after the wedding is the *portonnem* or *apovnemn*, a party at the bride's house. Symbolic of welcoming her and her new family to her own home, it is also a chance for the groom's extended family to check out the bride's house. Again, good food, music and dancing.

There is also another tradition that I vaguely remember. The bride's dowry and trousseau (*dennem*) including jewellery, pots and pans, crockery and cutlery, clothes, nightwear, and underwear are laid out on a bed for everyone to see. An old timer reminisces, 'It was very important that the bride hand-embroidered the pillowcases, handkerchiefs and all herself. Neighbours would come over to check the embroidery and the gold, even picking up the bangles in their hands to weigh and see how heavy they were.'

I have waved as women walk or scooter around the vaddo distributing the *vojem*—a basket of bananas and some traditional sweets (bol, dodol, doce)* taken around the village by the bride to meet and greet her new neighbours as she moves to a new home. Through this, they also get the opportunity to thank them for their help, ask for their blessings and befriend them.

---

* Goan sweets made with coconut, rice and jaggery.

I have discovered two syncretic wedding traditions over the last two years of living here. The *chuddo* (bangle) ceremony, is the first. A friend, Rowena, explains, 'The *cankonkar* (bangle seller) comes to the house and fits bangles on the bride's hands to the accompaniment of special songs sung for the occasion. It is hosted by the mama (the mother's brother). The bangles are green with yellow lines and symbolise married life.' I now understand why brides in their Western white wedding gowns wear green bangles. She goes on to explain that these bangles are supposed to be broken on the husband's grave.

The second one is *bhikarechi jevon*,* hosted in the homes where there is a wedding, a few days before the ceremony. Traditionally, families fed beggars and the poor to pray for the departed souls in the family. People now prefer to feed the destitute in old-age homes and orphanages. It was also done a few days after a person's passing to pray for his soul.

A neighbour, Salvador, nostalgically details wedding celebrations in Siolim in the 1960s when he was a young teenager and played the drums in a band. He explained, 'In those days, as there were no caterers to do the cooking and serving at weddings, there were *randpinns* (female Goan chefs) in every village who were called in or hired to prepare the wedding feast. All the women in the village would do the cooking supervised by these randpinns. The male chef was called a *meste*. Even the serving of snacks/meals during the ceremony in between the dancing, boys and girls would end up in a chain of people passing plates of food to the guests sitting all around the shamiana.'

---

* Konkani for beggar's feast.

He continues, 'In those days, our Goan weddings were a three to four-day event with a roce, followed the next day by a reception at the groom's house and the same repeated a day later at the bride's house (the portonnem). The nuptial mass was usually in the morning at the church. There were no halls for the reception, so they were held in the compound of the boy's house. Everyone from the vaddo and village was invited and expected to come. They would dig up a large area in front of the house and then throw water to dampen the soil. Two or three men would hammer it down with a heavy wooden block to compact the soil and make sure it was hard. Then it was ready to get a fine coat of cow dung. After the flooring was completed, a cloth *mattoh* (shamiana) was erected to cover the full area. Finally, just before the bridal couple made their entrance, talcum powder was sprinkled on the floor to make it smooth for dancing. The funniest part was that the girls who came for the wedding all dressed up with their high heels would poke holes and dig into the mud with all their ballroom dancing. So, the boys' suit pants from the knee down would be red with the *tambdi mati** that had come onto the girls' heels and the boys' suits, as they whirled their partners around the makeshift mud-cow-dung-powdered dance floor. We would set up the band most often in the balcao in the front of the house which served as a stage and play a couple of songs to announce to the villagers it was time to dress up and come. The band was truly acoustic with wind instruments such as trumpet, alto sax, tenor sax, double bass, guitar and a drummer. There was no electricity, so

---

* Konkani for red mud.

singers sometimes used a megaphone to amplify the sound and the big Petromax lamps that hung all over provided the light.'

The megaphones were also used to call people for the wedding, 'Kazar chol, chol.'*

Frazer Andrade, a collector and curator of Goan Christian art, explains wedding traditions, 'The mother of the bride would present her daughter with an Infant Jesus. It was crafted from wood, bone, ivory or silver and adorned with jewellery reminiscent of Indian cultural traditions, such as waistbands, anklets and bracelets. These Infant Jesuses bear a striking resemblance to the images of baby Krishna in the cradle. Artisans, both Hindu and newly converted Catholic, would sculpt these intricate creations to showcase the beautiful fusion of cultures. The bride-to-be was also gifted a rosary and a statue of the patron saint of her church. For example, in Siolim, it would be a statue of St Anthony.'

Frazer continues, 'Back then, young girls were required to master various stitching and embroidery techniques. There was a tradition tied to the bride's needlework skills— when there was a proposal, the prospective bride presented a meticulously stitched cloth sample known as the 'amostra da bordação'. The groom's family would then select a particular embroidery type from the sample, requesting the bride to create a decorative wall hanging bearing a portrait of the Sacred Heart of Jesus, the Immaculate Heart of Mary or a floral design.'

---

* Konkani for 'let's go for the wedding'.

Eating Goan

Most tourists and visitors don't experience Goan food beyond the ubiquitous fish thali. Goans have an extensive repertoire of vegetarian and vegan foods with lots of coconut. Each festival offers a wide variety of indigenous foods delicately cooked for the occasion using only seasonal fruits and vegetables. We tasted some of the traditional sweets for feasts—variations of three key ingredients (rice, coconut and jaggery)—godshe, von and alle belle (a rice pancake with a coconut and jaggery filling that is typically made for Shrove/Pancake/Fat Tuesday, the last day of feasting before fasting for Lent).

The jaggery for all Goan sweets needs to be the real and authentic madachem gud.* Making this dark coconut jaggery that comes from the coconut sap is another fading heritage which is getting expensive and harder to find. With our commitment to millets and becoming Goan, we ate tizan (a porridge made with nachni millets and coconut) often for breakfast along with embracing nachni† in dosas and chillas.

Over these past few years, we have tasted a vast assortment of Gaud Saraswat Brahmin (GSB) Hindu cuisine including alsande tonak, a rich coconut gravy with the local alsane (cowpeas), which we now make regularly. I have also tried the sasav, a ripe mango curry that we loved so much that we made it every week during the mango season. Other mouth-watering GSB delicacies we enjoy are the ambadeche

---

* Konkani for a local jaggery made from coconut palm sap. It is very dark brown, almost black and sold in pyramid-shaped blocks.
† Finger millet, ragi.

uddhamethi, a sweet-sour curry made with hog plum in coconut gravy, and of course, the popular kismoor (a dry prawn chutney). We have also relished ambadeche karam (a chutney made with the hog plum) and mangane, a kheer, for Diwali family celebrations with my school bestie Radha at her large joint family home in Miramar.

The lighter Goan fare inspired by Portuguese cooking styles referred to as Luso-Goan cuisine includes bakes and cakes. These dishes are delicately flavoured and some include a splash of wine, toddy, cashew and coconut. We love bol sans rival* and have tried to make our child-friendly version of amêijoas à bulhão pato.† When my four-year-old grandnephew, Samir, visited us from London with his mother, my niece, Mithika, he was always excited about buying and 'eating shells'. He loves the whole production of the dish—finding the clams in the Siolim market and watching them open as you sauté them with garlic and some home-grown herbs. Licking the shells to scoop the clam out, he collects all the shells and proudly shows how much he has eaten (not a lot). I don't use white wine in my preparation so that kids can also eat it. My bestie, Piki, is trying to preserve this Portuguese–Goan cuisine and has started a home catering enterprise. Her apa de camarao‡ and vegan unde com cogumelos§ for Kunal, and torta de choriço¶ for us are all legendary and to die for.

---

* A layered cashew cake with buttercream icing.
† Local clams cooked with white wine.
‡ A prawn stuffed pie localized with some toddy.
§ Portuguese for mushroom pies.
¶ Portuguese for Goan sausage pies.

My dear old friends, Annamaria and Milagres, who are rockstar Goan cooks, used to cook for me regularly when I first extended this house and visited from London. They make unbelievably authentic Goan food, which is becoming a scarce commodity in Goa. They have even passed the test of a very tough crowd here—my many cousins and friends—who gave a strong seal of approval to their varieties of fish, prawn curries and genuine sorpotel. The group included a discerning chef, Cousin Rui Madre Deus, who was a stickler for authentic Goan food and did not approve of it losing its original ingredients and flavours. Over the last few years, our housekeeper here, Reshma, has learned to cook Goan food, and Annamaria and Milagres have been busy. As a special treat, once a year at Christmas, they come over to conjure up their now famous sorpotel. For Christmas 2020, they were horrified by the idea of cooking soypotel for a vegan Kunal. 'Why won't he eat pork? Why this soya?' After Kunal's protracted explanation of animal rights, cruelty, methane gas and the environmental impact along with some old-fashioned begging, they acquiesced. Their soypotel turned out to be the pièce de résistance.

Annamaria advises me on choosing fresh fish in the Siolim fish market. While the whole fish-buying experience is hugely entertaining for her, it is humiliating for me. She guffaws at my lack of knowledge. 'All those stalls with those men selling all that big fish and many sizes of prawns they bring from the trawlers. They go out to fish at night. They put it on ice and bring it to sell in the market here,' she explains. When I assumed that I should trust the sweet old ladies, she laughed even louder and steered me clear of them, whispering, 'They mix stale with fresh fish.' Further corroborating Bharat's theory, he believes, 'Fisherwomen are the smartest, slickest salespeople on the planet. With such a perishable commodity, they will say anything. They have no conscience.' The Siolim fish market is a bustling place—it is where the locals meet to buy and sell their home-grown or freshly caught produce. You can see fishermen bringing in their fresh catch off their boats to sell most mornings. 'Don't go on Mondays and Thursdays,' Anna warns me. 'Hardly any fish in the market. Hindus don't eat on those days no.'

As time goes by, I am trying hard to learn to tell by looking at the gills if the fish is fresh or not and to speak Konkani. My bad Marathi helps a little but I have no ear for languages. When I go to the Siolim market, I practise by bargaining for fresh fish and vegetables while the women take pity and try not to laugh out loud.

Feasts and Festivals

During the summer holidays in early May every year, there is an annual celebration in the church compound that runs for three days to build community, raise funds, and support and nurture local talent. I enjoy the fancy dress, singing and dancing competitions, home-made delicacies and catching up with neighbours. There was a spectacular after-Covid fundraiser for the church in May 2022, when local legend Remo and his band, the Microwave Papadums, rocked the church compound in the melting heat. With mesmerizing energy and enthusiasm, he played his various guitars and the flute as he sang in English, Konkani and Hindi. Opening to his home crowd with his 'Ode to Siolim' and ending with his party favourite 'Maria Pitache', he brought the crowd to their feet.

The next day was the much looked-forward-to tiatr, a highlight on the Siolim cultural calendar. Even though I was a little sceptical when invited enthusiastically by a neighbour—as I thought I would not understand all the subtleties of Konkani—I decided to go along to try to appreciate the language and art form. The music, performances, powerful themes, social messages and satire were inspirational. There was a full orchestra, fancy costumes, slapstick action and outstanding singing. Hysterical, poignant and hard-hitting, it was a social commentary on the many evils that Goa is struggling with, including dysfunctional and separated families, property disputes, drugs and alcoholism. With this combination of French farce and Broadway musicals, maybe I would not miss the West End anymore.

Tiatr is an important part of Goan identity. As a child in Pune, I remember big black and white newspaper ads announcing Alfred Rose's tiatr performances in Pune. Journalist Frederick Noronha, who spends a lot of time and effort documenting this heritage performance art, explains, 'The tiatr was born amidst Goan diasporan communities in Bombay about 130 years ago. Its popularity later spread to and across Goa. Since the 1980s, Goa has become the epicentre of tiatr. Because of the sharply critical messages, regimes during and after colonial times have looked at tiatr with suspicion.'

My dogs are terrified and bark furiously when they hear these very loud vans fitted with loudspeakers going around the village announcing tiatrs, zatras and feasts or shouting out Covid-19 prevention and vaccination information.

Ganesh Chaturthi is, by far, the biggest festival in Goa—it is when the cities come to a standstill while everyone heads to the villages. Everything (including the schools, offices and shops) is closed, while ten days of festivities celebrate the birth of the elephant god Ganesh, son of Shiva and Parvati, who takes away obstacles. Ganesh celebrations in Goa also have a connection to mother nature as a *matoli** is suspended above the idol and decorated with a variety of typical seasonal wildflowers, fruits, leaves, gourds, coconuts and creepers. Traditionally, folks would forage in the forests for all of these, but today there are special markets that sell all you need to decorate your matoli. Lord Ganesha is worshipped with rituals, sweets (coconut modaks and neoris†) and celebrations and immersed in water on the last day. Rumour suggests that as the Ganesh idol leaves from the front door, fish comes in from the back door, reconfirming every Goan's devotion to fish. While Covid-19 threw a dampener on the festivities in the past few years, the loud music and firecrackers were back from 2022—my poor dogs and all the dogs across the state were terrified again.

The two other unique festivals I have seen celebrated only in Goa and on a grand scale are Shigmo at Holi and burning the demon, Narkasur, at Diwali.

The truly colourful and spectacular Shigmo is celebrated with special music, dancing, folklore, giant floats and colours. It marks the beginning of spring and each village has their own special rituals, dances and Shigmo celebrations.

---

* A canopy above the Ganesh idol.
† Traditional sweets made with rice flour, coconut and sugar. Modaks are steamed and neoris are deep fried.

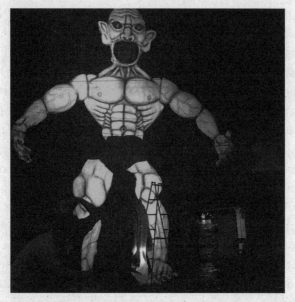

An effigy of Narkasur in Panjim, Diwali 2021

The day before Diwali, giant effigies of Narkasur are burnt at dawn to celebrate good winning over evil. Legend and mythology believe that in ancient times, the demon king Narkasur ruled the beautiful land of Gomantak* and was slain by Lord Krishna. On the sides of the roads in the weeks preceding Diwali, you see these gargantuan demons being made as families and communities creatively work together. With funds raised, materials sourced and fireworks stuffed, paints and papers are slapped on the structure. To celebrate this, a huge variety of deliciousness is conjured together with one main ingredient, fov (puffed rice). A few of the

---

* Ancient mythological name for Goa.

variations we have tried are dudhatle (cooked with milk), rosatle (with coconut milk) and kalile (with coconut and jaggery). We are invited with, 'Fov *khavpak yo aamger* [Come home to eat some fov]'

Friends visiting their family deities for auspicious occasions, births, weddings and new homes also drop in to visit us when they come to Goa. They make a special trip to visit Shantadurga, Mangeshi or their family goddess. While Covid-19 slowed them down, they have now returned with a renewed devotion to get blessings for new ventures.

Goa comes alive at Christmas. Siolim is lit up with strings of colourful, blinking lights lining the roads and vaddos. Stars are strung out and trees are decorated in front of houses. There is shopping for new clothes and shoes and elaborate sweet and cake making. Our vaddo has two huge community cribs with a life-size traditional nativity scene including shepherds, angels, farm animals and the three kings. There is often festive lighting and automation for the heads to move to the music while the carols are played. On Christmas Eve, everyone heads for midnight mass at St Anthony's church followed by cake, coffee and Christmas greetings.

Many travel across the country and the world to be home for Christmas. We always went to Pune to celebrate Christmas with my parents. Extended families get together for the traditional Christmas lunch. Beyond sorpotel and sannas, the lavish spread extends to a vast repertoire of festive dishes—delicately roasted chicken, ham, pulao, and assortment of trays of sweets and cakes. After a long lunch usually served closer to teatime, Christmas presents are exchanged. Later that evening, suited, booted, sequined, perfumed and made-up couples head out for the Christmas dance. A friend comes regularly from Dubai, 'I love being in Goa for Christmas, you can feel the Christmas spirit in the air with all the carols, the traditions and decorations.'

The Carnival is widely celebrated in the four-day build-up to Ash Wednesday*—the last few days of partying before the austerity and fasting of Lent. Panjim was and is party central with the streets decorated with colourful streamers. The carnival has its monarch, King Momo, who is a larger-than-life royal reigning over the festivities for four days. He also chooses a Queen and they bring drama and much excitement. The floats that meander down Panjim and other city streets are ruled over by King and Queen Momo and have strong political messages focused on drugs, pollution, casinos and mining. There are street dances, food, plenty of live music and drinking. Goans despair about how this carnival has become commercial and lost its original flavour over the years.

---

* Ash Wednesday is a holy day of prayer, fasting and abstinence in the Catholic Church. It is the first day of Lent, the six weeks of penitence that ends with Easter.

Living Local–Finding
My Go-To Places

My moment of victory towards claiming my Goan status was when my three words of spoken Konkani, 'Maka don di', got me the special rate for Goans at the newly opened Aguada Jail complex. It reopened in 2021 as an art and museum space designed by Goan architect Gerard de Cunha. We went in January 2023 to see Paresh Maity's 'Infinite Light' exhibit, which included gigantic installations and sculptures, gentle water colours and imposing oils. Each piece showcased Maity's mastery of the media.

The Aguada Jail complex has differentiated pricing for Goans, Indians, foreigners and senior citizens. The same goes for the refurbished Dona Paula jetty, which is free for Goans only.

In my continued quest to become a local, domiciled Goan, I have government documentation—a voter card, Aadhar card and driving licence (no easy achievement given how slow and corrupt life is here). And of course, a car with GA number plates and a two-wheeler licence. I hope I am now legally Goan beyond the emotion, ancestry and criteria on my own made-up 'Being Goan' list. I also make my own coconut oil, know all my living and dead relatives, go to more funerals than wedding masses, have joined a choir, and take my eating and drinking seriously.

The food here is a matter of honour and fierce pride. The legend of my discerning palate and my love for haute cuisine has now made me the 'go-to person' for family and friends looking for recommendations for everything from feni and sausages to the hippest gin bars and French cafes. Am I now the insider, complete with the stereotypical susegad lifestyle? If I am, then here is my real authentic local intel:

Fancy restaurants are popping up every week with different international cuisines and tourists visit only to relish the lavish spots. Though I absolutely love the variety of options available, I wish there was a range of authentic Goan food for tourists to try. How do we look at seasonal and local ways of including indigenous foods, millet, grains and veggies on our sophisticated tables? Can we think about more tambdi bhaji* and nachni† and less kale and quinoa on the menus? There are so many millets with such great flavours that are nutty and crunchy. In an attempt to ensure that tourists don't only eat butter chicken and Gujarati thalis but taste some authentic Goan food when they are here, in October 2023, the tourism minister made it mandatory to serve 'fish curry-rice' in beach shacks across Goa.

Every city, village and beach in Goa has their own unique ecosystem that is worth exploring. Each has

---

* Red amaranth, laal bhaji and laal maas.
† Ragi, finger millet.

impressive churches, chapels and temples. In a state that is geographically spread out and so rich in biodiversity, everywhere and every place is special. Soak it in. Lie on the beach or walk in the forest. Swim in the lake, the creek or the backwaters. Savour the moment. Why tire yourself out rushing around? However, tourists hit Goa and hit the road, zipping between the beaches, shacks, shops, cafés, bars and restaurants that they need to tick off on their Goa list.

Every time a tour agent, writer or social media influencer mentions a remote beach there is pushback from Goans. 'Please don't post, don't give away all our secrets. Tourists will go there, bring their trash and ruin it. Look at Morjim and Ashwem now.' We get the same request from neighbours who show us Siolim's secret walks and views. They make us promise not to take or post photos so that they remain a secret for Siolkars.

The south is less expensive and touristy. The north has become overpriced and overcrowded and is losing its Goan charm.

Over years of relocating, I have created a go-to list of people to call for recommendations for doctors, vets, groceries and restaurants. In Goa, I have a go-to list of cousins, old friends and neighbours who I call regularly. However, I realize that, often friends prefer to check with Google, anonymous Trip Advisor or Amazon recommendations from random strangers (who are probably not even human), over the real local experience. Alternatively, they prefer sponsored and paid-for lists. Maybe we are being controlled by AI already. I know that Apple, Google and Facebook know too much about me and are trying every trick in the book to manipulate me, my shopping and travel choices and decisions, but I still try to have real human connections.

Staying Local

As you have read, when we got here in June 2020, it was pouring rain and we were coming out of a very strict three-month lockdown. While we were cautious about leaving the security of our home, we wanted to embrace the lack of restrictions and take a breather from our computer screens when there was a break from the torrential rain. Soon, we started driving to Uddo, the backwater beach here in Siolim to catch the splendour of those spectacular monsoon sunsets, sip a sundowner and support local businesses as they were all struggling. We were welcomed with our standing orders—a table with a view, a round of local beers and plates of their outstanding onion rings.

The best sausages and vinegar are available right here in the vaddo. Dominic's sausages (from our vaddo) are now so popular with friends and family that I have a standing order of three kilos a month to be picked up and shipped out. Unfortunately, poor Dominic has lost ownership of his sausages and they are popularly known as Michelle's sausages! However, you can't decide that you want the sausages tomorrow. You need up to a minimum of two days' notice. When you call, the response could be, 'No sausages now. No time to dry them. Call after ten days, ok?' But they are well worth the wait. When friends and family drop in on a quick trip to Goa and hope to pick up these local delicacies, they are often disappointed.

The special tang of the sorpotel and vindaloo comes from the typical, home-made vinegar fermented from palm toddy that Goans treasure and smuggle to all corners of the world along with sausages. A popular word for an Indian curry across continents, a vindaloo has more to do with the level of heat than the taste. In the UK, a fiery curry is referred to as vindaloo while the original flavour has been lost in translation. The dish comes from a Portuguese Carne de vinha d'alhos, which is a meat dish—typically pork marinated in wine and garlic. The dish was Goanized using local toddy vinegar and spices. To get the authentic vindalho flavour, it's important to use this specific vinegar. When the dish was exported, both the name and the flavour were anglicised to 'vindaloo'.

An angel in Siolim makes bebinca for the Gods—my mouth waters just thinking of that heavenly flavour with a touch of nutmeg. The reason I am not sharing their names and details is that I don't have them myself—I have a friend who has a friend. There are levels of insiders here.

My neighbour, Tanya, sources delicious xacuti and samarche masala. Her Siolim supplier exports to the Goan community across the world. She also recommended Siolim-based caterer, Jeffrey, who makes mouth-watering beef roast and croquettes. He brings the food over on his scooter in his own dabbas, all fresh and flavourful, and returns a few days later to pick up his dabbas and asks for our feedback. Rosie, another neighbour, makes home-made sorportel, samarche kodi, and vegan sweets like von and dodol. Her sannas are very light and absolutely delicious as she makes them with the special Goan toddy.

Vaddo Women's Self-Help Groups

The Porto Vaddo self-help women's group had a stall during the pandemic and our dear old friends, Annamaria and Milagres, who are outstanding Goan cooks, were part of it. We loved the cutlets, chicken spring rolls, prawn chops, chana dose, bolinhas and the Sunday special sannas.

Now, the Milan self-help group sells their home-made treats in the church compound on Saturday evenings and Sundays after mass. They have all the staples—fresh, delicious and reasonably priced. We have enjoyed their puran polis (you can take the boy out of Pune), the Tavasali (cucumber cake), and the patoleo and donne (coconut, jaggery and rice flour but steamed in a jackfruit leaf instead of turmeric).

When we got here in June 2020, I was still living my Marie Antoinette days, eating cake every day, not knowing this pandemic would last for years. We reconnected with old friends—Lily, Yves and Rishad Braganza, and they provided us with sweet treats every weekend, for all birthdays and any and every celebration. All their cakes, cupcakes, desserts and especially their lemon tarts, are to die for. We use our own dabbas and cake boxes to minimize packaging waste.

Agnelo, Santa Cruz, Jackin and St Anthony's bakeries offer regular Goan sweets, puffs, croquettes and cakes with their smiling service and village news. Some sell fresh sandwiches and samosas too. We often order and carry them on our drives to Mumbai.

Green Chokrees is a Siolim-based grocery selling organic, environmentally and ethically sourced products—veggies, grains, seeds, spices and spreads. Jasmine and Dita, its founders, are well-organized and have an interesting list for Siolim and north Goa delivery twice a week. Their delivery person, Amar, comes on a scooter to deliver directly to our home.

Zero Posro have an electric rickshaw with a no-plastic, no-waste delivery system. Jonah, its founder, who grew up in Siolim, steers the souped-up custom-made rickshaw and delivers organic groceries to your door. You can use your kitchen containers to buy and store them, eliminating the need for any packaging.

Ethico is also working towards sustainability with its no-plastic policy. The store has a range of grains, snacks, coffee, home products and furniture, and is a co-working space. The owners, Indranil and Raabia, use their space as a collection centre to sort and recycle dry waste including glass, plastic, e-waste, etc., a critical cause as we continue to drown in the garbage that is thrown on the sides of the streets in Siolim.

Siolim-based popular cheesemaker, Swiss Happy Cow, makes a wide assortment of cheeses. They retail in supermarkets across Goa. Divya recommends the brie and camembert and I recommend the mozzarella and the kombucha.

The wholesale dry fruit store in Siolim, Altaf, has a range of cashews, dry fruits, chillis and masalas.

Rockstar Local Entrepreneurs beyond Food

In October 2020, when we realized masks were here to stay and needed stylish and strong masks, we met Savio Jon, the internationally acclaimed fashion designer who was born and brought up right here in Siolim. Savio Jon has set up an elegant boutique and studio in his Fernandes vaddo home. Along with his line of boho chic aspirational clothes, he has an exclusive collection of knick-knacks and bric-a-brac that he has chosen with his exquisite taste from his travels around the state, country and world. He is always generous, warm and welcoming.

Dr Astrid Almeida, in next-door Cunchelim, has saved Rusty's and Roo's lives during grave emergencies when our dogs have gotten into life-threatening fights with each other. On separate occasions, Haruki bit off Roo's ear and Roo took a chunk out of Rusty's back. Only because of our two amazing vets, Dr Almeida's and Dr Meher Abadian's care and commitment, did our dogs survive and continue to be healthy. Though they have not been able to help us figure out why our dogs are so crazy.

WAG here provides shelter and medical facilities for every kind of bird and animal and has also helped us with dog emergencies.

In March 2021, after a year of eating cake and drinking gin, I decided I needed to get strong. During the pandemic, I could work and socialize but could not do yoga online. Hence, I desperately needed to sort out my frozen shoulder, knee and joint problems—the many joys of old age. The orthopaedic doctor recommended Pilates, but after my classes at Triyoga in London back in 2010, I could not find a teacher that fit into my regular pre-Covid schedule. Luckily, Keya, who lives around the corner in Siolim, is a brilliant teacher. She is strict, pushes hard and keeps me focused. I am getting strong and lean (not just mean).

I also go next door to Tanya's Space for morning *Hatha* yoga with Sara thrice a week, who is a great teacher and an activist for women's rights in Iran.

In Siolim, you will see plenty of 'bikes on rent', 'rooms available' or 'call for taxi' signs. Many of my neighbours run local businesses, so if we need a taxi, there are options. It is the same with motorbike, scooter or tempo rental, which helped when Divya needed to move furniture to the south of Goa.

Spick and Span Car Wash offers great service. They opened in 2022 in a convenient location on the Siolim Marna road and have instantly become so popular that you often have to wait to get your car washed.

How could I get through this account without a mention of the local liquor store, Ferns? Always smiling, Greg, the owner, gives us a healthy discount and sources the variety of strange, new gins that I ask him for. Most of his other customers pick up a quart of whisky or rum, a bag of chips or nuts. Then there is me. When he asked Kunal if we run a restaurant, Kunal smiled and calmly said, 'No, my mom drinks a lot.' It was a pandemic after all.

Bharat has also spent fulfilling evenings at the local dive in the market, Amancio. There, we have knocked back a few Old Monks and cokes alongside the local labour after their hard days' work with some peanuts, all for a princely sum of Rs 100. Over the last two years, good old Siolim Taar has started to become gentrified. The tiny bars with Goan uncles hanging out in the evenings for their feni shot and gossip, and the large stores selling cloth and fishing supplies, are now glamourized with a Japanese restaurant, organic handmade stores and a big Russian store.

Mahalaxmi chemist and many more in Siolim sell all the medicines we need. Mahalaxmi also sells veterinary supplies and medicines so it saves us a trip to Mapusa or Panjim.

As I continue with my quest to live and buy local, and never leave Siolim, there is one anecdote that I must retell. I was here visiting from London over the Christmas of 2009 to set up this house and stock up on groceries for our stay. I

had made a run to the Mapusa market and still needed some
stuff. My late aunt, Sister Mary Ann (aka my guardian angel)
had been recently transferred to Siolim and was helping me
sort out my domestic responsibilities—cooking, cleaning the
well and fixing the pump. I had lost touch with shopping at
the local posro* while shopping at Marks and Spencer and
Waitrose in London and could not get my head around the
local market selling fresh chicken, beef and pork only on
Wednesdays and Sundays at the church square. I was not
used to having to ask for the stuff I required instead of picking
it up from the shelf myself. Sister Mary Ann recommended
the popular posro, Pangam, at the Tinto,† as he was both
reasonable and reliable. I went there and looked sceptically at
his overstuffed, disorganized shop and all that he had to sell,
with my London supermarket lens, not being able to believe he
could meet my needs better than Marks and Spencer Foods. I
was fascinated and stared open-mouthed across the counter—
Uddesh Pangam and his family members attended to at least
six customers at any given moment, managing to chat, enquire
about their family, find, sell, wrap in newspaper and bill them
for all the things they needed. I had forgotten how these small
shops work beyond products and offer personalized service.
As I watched in awe at all the buying and selling of tea,
detergents, rice and biscuits, a foreigner burst in and asked for
olives. I thought to myself with my narrow London mindset,
'You think he has olives here in this run-down village store?'
Without batting an eyelid, Uddesh looked at him and asked,
'Black or green?' I was sold. He had everything I needed for

---

* Konkani for the grocer or corner store.
† Village marketplace.

any kind of food I wanted to cook. Since that day, I have been a loyal customer and am greeted with a warm smile, a familiar nod and a helping hand with my heavy bags.

Water Sports

When my sister Ingrid came to visit at the end of January 2021, she was very keen to go kayaking with her friends who run an adventure tourism company, Adventure Breaks, out of Bambolim. They offer kayaking, sailing experiences and trekking.

Since I wanted to stay local, we went kayaking down the Siolim backwater. I learnt that kayaking here is highly dependent on the tides—you can kayak only during high tide to experience some of the mangroves and mysteries of the river. In early March 2021, the four of us went with friends on a more ambitious trip that included standup paddleboarding (SUP) on the Chapora River. It was a blast to be able to swim, SUP and kayak right here with Konkan Explorers.

A couple of places in Morjim and Ashwem offer a range of water sports including surfing and kite surfing.

In the monsoons, we headed to swim in the quarries in Mandrem in the north. Abandoned quarries fill up with water and form natural pools. They are becoming popular with Goa settlers and curated tourist experiences in the monsoons include a quarry swim.

Sports

Goans love football. If you are here during the Indian Soccer League (ISL) season from October to February, do go to the

Fatorda stadium and support FC Goa. The atmosphere is electric with bands, bugles, songs and chants. Wear the FC Goa shirt and wave the flag.

Eco-Initiatives in Goa

Terra Conscious is a team of passionate conservationists working towards empowering the local community through responsible marine, education-oriented coastal experiences. In March 2021, we went with founders Pooja and Roshan on a responsible dolphin-watching boat experience from the Candolim jetty and learnt about their work in sustainable tourism and engaging local communities in conservation. I even made it to a documentary on France24 as the crew was interviewing Terra Conscious on that day.*

Khoj-aao! curates offbeat, unique experiences for nature lovers and adventurers. All their experiences are environmentally and socially conscious, engage local communities and support both local and global conservation efforts. We have been on a nature trail with founders Pooja and Bipin along the Chapora River here in Siolim, on a bird walk on the Socorro plateau and a sunset bird-watching boat ride on the Chapora.

Dr Maryanne Lobo is an Ayurvedic doctor from a family of healers. She, with her husband, Roussel, leads 'Plant Walks Goa' and teaches you how to recognize and forage for medicinal plants and herbs. You experience forgotten

---

* Diya Gupta and Thomas Denis, 'Revisited - Indian State of Goa Continues to Attract Dreamers from around the World', France 24, 16 July 2021, https://www.france24.com/en/tv-shows/revisited/20210716-indian-state-of-goa-continues-to-attract-dreamers-from-around-the-world.

food and medicine and learn original, sustainable village community practices. She offers walks in Siolim, Assagao, Mapusa and on the Soccoro Plateau.

Sensible Earth does remarkable work in reusing, recycling and community building. They claim, 'It is a local Goan movement aimed at providing a sustainable alternative to single-use plastic in Goa and someday, globally. #MakaNakaPlastic aims to solve three crucial problems, namely the environmental damage caused by single-use plastic, the carbon emissions created by the fast fashion industry and lastly, the female unemployment percentage, which has worsened due to the COVID-19 pandemic.' They operate out of Salvador du Mundo.

Living Heritage Foundation is working towards the conservation and preservation of trees through documentation and litigation. Sadly, so many of these old, benevolent beauties are being culled in the name of development. Founder Mohan Kumar explains, 'Since its inception, our primary focus has been trees. We've tried to advocate against cutting through video content, RTIs and litigation.' In October 2023, they collaborated on a Goa's green brigade initiative to map and gather data of trees on public land and private forests in Assagao and Panjim.*

Next door in Vagator, with an outpost in Rabbit Hole restaurant in Siolim, Vijaya Pais' initiative, the Good Karma Treasure Shop, is cultivating a thrifting culture. They accept and sell pre-loved clothes by marketing them on social

---

* If you are looking to save Goa's rich natural heritage and biodiversity, do support, volunteer and donate to the Goa Foundation at http://goafoundation.org.

media and donate a percentage of the proceeds to support NGOs working across Goa.

Many local Facebook and WhatsApp groups facilitate recycling and thrifting by sharing used clothes, household stuff, plants, books, seeds, gardening and composting supplies, and expertise. Excellent resources, they are all trying to reduce waste.

Looking for a Bit of History and a Touch of Culture?

Historic places

The historic churches of Old Goa and the temples in Ponda are notable for their architecture, history and the devotion they inspire.

The huge heritage houses in Salcette give you a taste of the grandeur of the lavish colonial lifestyles. It is worth making a trip and booking a tour, which helps with their costs of upkeep.

A quick, fun must-do for tourists is a walk around Panjim church and through the now popular Latin quarter, Fontainhas. The architecture, boutiques, bars and cafes make you feel you are in Southern Europe. But its quick gentrification is coming at a cost. While there are more employment opportunities, there are also crowds and noise. When we visit friends who live there, they are struggling with genuine issues of traffic, parking, crowds and privacy as there are often Instagrammers at their doorstep proposing or taking photos. Along with a recent news story when a resident threw water at tourists, some have installed spikes on their steps as callous tourists are leaning, stepping and putting their shoes on newly painted doors and walls. Residents there complain, 'How can we live here peacefully now? Tourists are everywhere trying to take photos, parking in front of our doors.'

A great spot for a quick drive is the Reis Magos Fort. Walk around the beautifully renovated fort, experience some history and take in the sea breeze and the view. Other forts with history and panoramic views that are worth hiking to are Tiracol on the northern tip and Cabo de Rama on the southern tip. Do also drop in at the newly renovated Aguada Jail Complex. It has great views, lots of history and interesting art.

Goa Heritage Action Group are working tirelessly to preserve Goan heritage and culture. They have regular walks, heritage weeks and festivals in April and November every year. I learnt about Goa's history and architecture through their informative walks and sessions at the November 2022 heritage festival. Their mission is 'to protect Goa's natural, cultural and built heritage; to take Goa towards a sustainable, eco-friendly future to the benefit of all the stakeholders; to protect Goa's biodiversity for future generations to enjoy; and to instil an element of pride in Goa's heritage so as to slow down emigration of young Goans from the state.'*

The Jesuit Xavier Centre for Historical Research in Porvorim, 'is designed to serve as a base for scholarly research in the history and cultural heritage of India, with particular emphasis on contemporary cultural and social

---

* 'Our Mission', Goa Heritage Action Group, http://goaheritageaction group.org/mission/.

issues affecting the state of Goa'.* They host lectures, book launches, exhibitions and workshops.

I was elated to finally experience the exquisite originals of Angelo da Fonseca in March 2023 that was curated by art historian, artist and author, Savia Viegas. Over the years, she has toiled to bring him into public consciousness by curating exhibitions, holding lectures, writing a book and nurturing children to draw, paint and appreciate his art.

The poignancy, elegance and gentleness of Fonseca's vast portfolio are powerful. He was way ahead of his time and almost 100 years later, we are trying to catch up.

His wife, Ivy, and daughter, Yessonda, lived next door to my grandparents in Pune where I grew up. Ingrid and Yessonda went to nursery school and played together. Ingrid has a portrait of herself as a five-year-old by this leading-edge artist. As a child, I had neither the understanding nor the appreciation of his pioneering style. I took the Indianized Madonna and child for granted and did not question the colonialism of religion or how using images of white, blond, blue-eyed Mary and Jesus was propagating the European domination of culture and religion. As I have been reflecting on my identity, I appreciate the allure of his art and how his portrayal of the big, dark-eyed, saree-clad Madonna and child had helped me relate to a usually ritualistic, European, male-dominated religion.

Fundação Oriente Delegation was inaugurated in 1995 in Goa in the historical Fontainhas area of Panjim. It supports the teaching of Portuguese, conservation of cultural heritage, historical and artistic research and scholarships, and organizes festivals, concerts, exhibitions, seminars,

---

* 'XCHR – Xavier Centre of Historical Research – Research Institute in Goa', https://xchr.in/.

conferences and events. It also has a permanent exhibition of selected works of Goa's famous artists, the Trinidades. Worth a visit to see these fine paintings.

Sunaparanta is a strong advocate for the arts in Goa. It provides a working and exhibition space, grant funding initiatives, and infrastructural and creative support for projects. Located in a lovely old house on the picturesque Altinho hills of Panjim, Sunaparanta also hosts book releases, lectures, musical, theatre and film presentations.* It is always educational to see the exhibits and listen to the discussions that are held.

The Charles Correa Foundation, with its office in Fontainhas, offers a range of discussions and incubations around architecture, design and urban planning.

Do check on social media or the newspapers if you are interested in learning about art, culture, design, conservation and architecture at any of these places.

Kala Academy in Campal, the impressive Charles Correa-designed cultural centre on the banks of the Mandovi, hosts a thriving arts community and teaches music, dance, drama, fine art, folk art and literature. It also has a variety of classes, conferences and festivals. It is currently closed for renovation and had a serious roof collapse (fortunately, no human was injured). We hope it will reopen soon.

Music

The charming Madragoa is the world's first house of Fado and Mandó. A small but dramatically designed space in

---

* Sunaparanta Goa Centre for the Arts, https://www.sgcfa.org, last accessed 20 October 2023.

Panjim (ironically right across from the blinding casino lights), it is working hard to preserve and propagate Luso–Goan culture with its enchanting fado–mando nights, delicious snacks and drinks. It is a must-visit. I loved listening to and learning from Goa's nightingale, the talented, always charming and smiling, Sonia Shirsat. They announce their concerts on their Facebook page.

Sounds From Goa does 'heritage home concerts' and offers 'traditional music, folk dances, authentic cuisine and beverages in a heritage home in Benaulim in the South and Assagao in the North'. It is your chance to experience Indo–Portuguese culture all in one place.

The Stuti Choir, as well as other children and adult choirs, promote sacred choral music in historic churches and locations. Listening to these choirs in churches is always a moving experience.

The Stuti choral ensemble was founded by the then parish priest of the St Inez Church in Panjim, Father Eufemiano Miranda, in 2009, to revive the choral music tradition in Goa. It is now directed by Parvesh Java. They performed Brahms Requiem in churches across Goa in October 2023 with a chorus of 100 strong singers, talented soloists, pianists and the Stuti strings ensemble. An emotional experience, their concerts are free, allowing everyone to access and experience classical music.

In March 2023, Stuti had an open call for anyone who wanted to learn to sing and I auditioned. Parvesh, beyond being a gifted pianist and conductor, is an inspirational and patient teacher. He can tell every single voice in a crowded room and knows precisely who is on and off key. To explain the level of my singing, if the main Stuti choir are at a PhD level, then I am at the kindergarten level. To ensure that we learn to sing, he very generously set up the Stuti Academy choir. I am an alto and am persevering to hold a note. It is one more notch on my belt to being a good Goan. I look forward to the practices on Monday and Thursday evenings at Kamra, a traditional Goan house, which has been repurposed into a contemporary practice and performance space in Porvorim. Kamra also hosts intimate classical music concerts.

Child's Play India Foundation (www.childsplayindia. org) teaches violin, viola, cello, double bass, recorder flute, piano and choir to disadvantaged children across Goa. It was founded by Dr Luis Dias in 2009 to transform the lives of young people through music. They have an orchestra, Camerata Goa, as well as choirs for children and adults. They hold regular classical music performances, and it is always inspiring and enchanting to listen to them. They advertise their performances in newspapers, on their website and social media.

Museums

The Museum of Christian Art (MoCA) in Old Goa is a must-visit. Located in the perfect, peaceful location on the picturesque Holy Hill in Old Goa in the seventeenth-century Convent of Santa Monica, the museum has contemporary technology, lighting and archiving. The art objects at MoCA are renowned for their antiquity and distinct Indo-Portuguese influence.* Uncle Nasci is one of the key people

---

* 'Museum of Christian Art', https://www.museumofchristianart.com/about-us#people.

behind this state-of-the-art upgrade and every time you talk
to him, he is understandably pleased and proud. For me, it
is a spiritual and educational place. I have learnt a lot from
the curator, Natasha Fernandes, and volunteers through
workshops, walks, performances and lectures. Their
monthly heritage walks are educational and immediately
sell out whenever they are advertised.

Subodh Kerkar's Museum of Goa (MOG) in Pilerne
holds an impressive, permanent contemporary art collection
and installations. In late 2022, Wendy Amanda Coutinho
curated a month-long exhibition titled '0832', celebrating
the creative spirit of the Goan diaspora. The prominent
artists whose work was featured included Sonia Rodrigues
Sabharwal (who has a mural at India's recently opened
Parliament). It is a vibrant centre for discussion and
activism with a packed calendar of exhibitions, workshops,
lectures, events, screenings and openings around art, history
and the environment. MOG hosts Sunday morning talks
and discussions curated by Nilankur Das of Thus.* that
encourage critical thought on environmental and social
issues affecting Goa and Goans.

Houses of Goa showcases the different aspects of Goan
houses and explains how they were the prime expression
of the Goan identity. The impressive physical structure in
laterite was built as a traffic island in Torda, Salvador-do-
Mundo by Goan architect Gerard da Cunha. It also houses

---

* Thus. is an organisation that looks to establish and encourage this
  critical questioning culture by identifying and organizing venues and
  curating the presentation of ideas that are at the intersection of art,
  activism, innovation and inspiration.

a Mario Miranda gallery. Worth a visit if you are interested in Goan architecture.

Goa Chitra, labelled as the ultimate museum of Goan ethnography, is a personal collection of hundreds of artefacts. The entry ticket includes an enthusiastic guide who walks you through the museum's three sections. In some ways, it is less museum and more agglomeration as there could be things from many centuries in one exhibit.

Carpe Diem is an eclectic art space in a heritage house in Majorda, which supports the artistic community through exhibitions, residences, film screenings, book launches and discussions. It was there that we saw the award-winning artist Damodar Madgaonkar's powerful portrayal of popular Konkani proverbs in April 2023.

I hardly ever get to Calangute these days, but Litterati offers a comprehensive selection of books, discussions, film screenings and literary events.

Street Art

Beyond the art galleries and museums in London, I started looking for art on the streets after a few walking tours in the Shoreditch Brick Lane neighbourhood. I marvelled at these detailed, large murals and tags in public spaces where they risked being painted over by the authorities or the residents.

Along with the rest of the world, I followed Banksy's brilliance and insolence, as he chose to remain anonymous and use his art as political and social commentary. Since then, in every city I have lived or visited, I have looked for street art—Mumbai, Delhi, Berlin, Sao Paulo or San Francisco.

In Panjim, I was affected by Solomon Souza's bold and imposing portraits on prominent walls. He is Goa's legendary modernist painter, F.N. Souza's* grandson. Curious about this project and the heroes portrayed, I learnt that they were part of the Serendipity Arts Festival 2019 Munda Goa exhibit, curated by writer, photographer and curator Vivek Menezes. I recognized some of the icons— Lata Mangeshkar (India's favourite voice), Sonia Shirsat (queen and ambassador of Fado) and Rita Faria (the first Asian to win the Miss World title in 1966 and the first Miss World winner to qualify as a doctor). Sadly, her mural in Campal has already been painted over—another reminder of how ephemeral the medium is. I had to look up others to understand their importance and influence—Mary D'Souza Sequeira, the first Indian to represent the country at the Olympics in two sports—hockey and track and field, and Sita Valles, a Marxist revolutionary of Goan origin who fiercely fought Portuguese colonialism in Angola. This Solomon Souza ICON project has twenty-four portraits honouring Goan athletes, musicians, artists, and writers, and keeps their memories alive in public spaces across North Goa. It is worth a trip to find them all.

There are tour companies that offer thoughtful walks and experiences, slow travel alternatives to the popular mass tourism. They help tourists visiting Goa to understand the unique culture, heritage and traditions beyond the beaches, and offer income to the guides and hosts. In a symbiotic

---

* Francis Newton Souza was born in Saligao, Goa, and was a founder member of the Progressive Artists Group that is largely responsible for shaping the Modern Art movement in India.

relationship with the locals, Soul Travelling, Make it Happen and Urbanaut are all promoting community tourism as well.

Festivals

I have attended world-class festivals here in Goa.

In November every year since 2004, the International Film Festival of India (IFFI) has put Goa on the world cinema map and routinely brings in a variety of films, writers and critics.

Serendipity, India's largest multidisciplinary arts festival, is held in Goa in mid-December. Over the years, it has been inspirational to see the sheer spectacle, diversity and dimension of performances and installations. It includes every art form in intricate detail with impeccable taste and style. We have experienced music (classical, folk, rock, pop and fusion), art, photography, theatre, martial arts, dance, culinary arts, film and heritage arts, and I have learnt so much from it.

The Goa Art and Literature Festival (GALF), started in 2010, is co-curated by Damodar Mauzo and Vivek Menezes. Organized by the International Centre Goa and Goa Writers Group, it brings writers, artists and musicians to Goa with a strong focus on Goan literature and diaspora. GALF is an important stop on the Indian literary festival circuit.

Originally held on the Monte Hill in Old Goa overlooking the Mandovi River, the Monte festival in February, supported by the Fundação Oriente, promotes sacred and fusion music and dance. We have enjoyed world-class Goan and international performances.

The D.D. Kosambi Festival of Ideas facilitates critical and relevant public lectures in Goa.

I often wonder how these festivals support films, arts, artists and activists at the grassroots level in the villages and cities of Goa. Do Goans attend in large numbers? Are they a part of the planning and implementation, bringing employment, opportunity, and ideas to and from Goa? Are Goans interested in participating? There are almost distinct sets of arty events and festivals catering to different expectations. I recently overheard, 'All these other festivals are just an excuse to come to Goa. It is outside interests being served here. Not for us locals.'

Historically, villages have feasts and festivals promoting community, culture, seasonal fruit, food and local music. Recently, there has been a revival of festivals trying to bring back traditions and history with a modern dimension. Festekar Marius Fernandes has been working tirelessly to make them self-sustaining and non-commercial. I went to the historical island of Divar's famous 400-year-old Bonderam heritage walk he curated in August 2022 and Pilerne's Mattiche Fest in October 2022—the food, history and community spirit were commendable.

Community Markets

At the warm, weekly Tuesday 'Made in Saligao' market, they build community and support local home businesses selling plants, veggies, food, wine, scrunchies, jewellery, pottery and music. Pilerne's community market is on Thursdays in the church compound with the same warm village feeling that promotes culture, commerce and community. Again, let's hope they remain grassroots and genuine and don't become commercial or political so that the traditions survive.

My Favourite Beaches

I am often asked about beaches. We started going to Ashwem in 2009 and it now has a very special place in my heart. We have seen how it has turned from pristine and isolated to another heaving, hopping party place. Even with its rows of shops selling beachwear and dreamcatchers, hawkers and tourists haggling over jewellery and massages, we manage to find windows to enjoy the peace. The excitement and anticipation of crossing over the creek, not sure if the water will be high or low, has a reassuring effect on my soul. Walking sweet Neo (our first family dog) there in 2013 and now, of course, the crazy Haruki who swims and plays there, bring me joy.

Morjim is also a go-to beach because it is closer and we can take Haruki there more regularly. Over the years, he seems to have gotten to know most of the dogs there, so that keeps the fights and the bites to a minimum.

In September 2021, when Divya moved to teach in an international school in Chaudi, Cancona, and lived near Colomb Beach between Palolem and Patnem, we discovered the pristine beaches of the deep south. Talpona and Galgibag are magical and isolated with the freshly caught seafood (oysters, crabs) as an added attraction.

Wildlife

Olive Ridley Turtles

Olive Ridley turtles head to the shores of Goa to nest from January to March, usually to Morjim and Mandrem in the North and Galgibag and Talpona in the south, which are now protected natural habitats. My naturalist friend Aparna explains, 'The turtle lays about 200 eggs between January and March, with an incubation period of about 60 days. The Forest Department puts up enclosures to protect the eggs from natural predators and from being trampled upon by humans. The hatching is monitored, ensuring that at least 70–80 per cent of the hatchlings get into the sea, guided by infrared light.'

Salim Ali Bird Sanctuary

You can take the ferry early in the morning to get to Chorão. Once there, hire a bird-watching boat along the mangroves to spot the rich variety of birds in the season and otters too.

Cotigao Wildlife Sanctuary

This peaceful sanctuary has dense deciduous forests and flowing water deep in Canacona on the border of Karnataka. There are plenty of opportunities for bird and animal spotting, and walking on clearly defined nature trails. The butterfly park is a unique attraction. My birder friend, Aparna, continues 'I have seen Goa's state butterfly, the diaphanous Malabar Tree Nymph, gliding over flowers, as well as the state bird, the yellow-throated bulbul.'

Cotigao is also where the indigenous Velip and Kunbi communities live. A few organizations offer sensitive experiences of their indigenous food and culture.

Restaurants

Here is my list (Divya put it together for fun when her college friends visited in February 2021). Since then, it has organically grown with the momentum of new restaurants exploding and the demand for a list of local recommendations. However, it is exhausting for us as whoever visits or moves here immediately becomes the resident authority, so they insist on informing us about the best places to go in Goa. There are always two questions—'Do you know?' or the opposite 'You don't know?'

Notable exceptions on our list are the five most popular restaurants that you will see on every Goa restaurant list, which we believe are tourist traps. Another warning—there are plenty of new restaurants opening every day with average food and service, which only have their Instagrammable locations to brag about. Beware!

Also, before heading out, please call and or/look up places on social media before you visit them as they may or may not be open. While some may be closed for private parties, some may not have survived with escalating costs of real estate or may be closed during the monsoon.

Siolim

Uddo: An outdoor beach shack where one can enjoy sundowners with an amazing view, great fries and onion rings.

Amancio Classic and Bar: Authentic Goan food that is local and affordable. I recommend the prawn balchao. On Tuesday nights, they also have live music.

Davides: Tasty home-style Italian pizza and pasta.

Cafe Pravin: Authentic Goan bhaji pao breakfast—fantastic bhaji pao, buns, fried chilli and shira.

Shiori: Japanese food with contemporary design and décor.

Coco Thai: Homestyle Thai street food, warm place. We love their greasy spring rolls, wings and the tangy tamarind steamed fish.

Navtara: Go here for a regular Udupi fix or Goan bhaji pao.

Panjim

Fontainhas

Antonio's: Chef Pablo Miranda's fabulous Goan fusion tapas and great cocktails. Nice vibe—warm and welcoming. My favourites include the mushroom and truffle rissois, the solantlem and the osso buco. My dogs are happy when I go as I bring them back big bones to chew on.

Makutsu: Also from Pablo is the genuine Japanese yakitori right next door.

Joseph's Bar: Quaint hipster Goan bar (popular on Instagram). Everyone tries the tambde rossa here—a feni cocktail with kokum juice and sliced chilli.

For the record: Vinyl bar with cool feni cocktails and jazz.

Horseshoe: Authentic, Luso-Goan food with old-world charm. The owner is the chef and a legend. We love his preparation of fresh clams in white wine.

Miski Bar: Local Goan taverna with casual food and drinks.

Venite: Charming décor with authentic Goan food. The fish is always good.

Petiscos: Nice bar, drinks, cocktails and finger food. They sometimes have live music.

Black Sheep Bistro/Black Market: Prahlad and Sabreen Sukhthankar are talented restaurateurs who have created this classy restaurant with amazing food. Their truffle mac and cheese is my favourite and they have many enticing cocktails to pick from.

Ritz Classic (three places in Panjim): Great fish thali.

Konkni Kanteen: Goan food and thali.

Café Bhosale/Café Tato: Authentic Goan breakfast—bhaji pao and fried chilli.

Padaria Prazeres: All their baked goods—focaccias, bagels, Berliners and sandwiches—are delicious. The pastels de nata are so legendary that you could be in Portugal. Bharat believes their egg salad sandwiches to be the best in the world.

Peep Kitchen: Popular with Goans as well as local and national celebs, including Sachin Tendulkar.

Copper Leaf: Popular thali, same as the original in Porvorim.

Anand Ashram: The OG fish thali in a poky place.

The Goan Room: This small place is in a convenient location in Dona Paula with real Goan food.

Sea Shells (Siridao): Nice view, vibe and Goan food. Sometimes, there is live music.

Fisherman's Wharf: Central location, Goan food and live music.

Perfect Bakery: Love their prawn patties and sausage rolls (these are not pigs in a blanket, but Goan chorizo baked in a bread roll.)

Café Central (Panjim and Porvorim): The absolute best onion biscuits, mushroom samosas and shankarpali.

Romeos: Fresh beef samosas, bols sans rival and apa de camarao on order.

D'Silva's: OG place for cutlet pao.

Porvorim

Café Bhosale: Authentic Goan breakfast. The original branch is in Panjim.

Ritz Classic: OG fish thali and Goan food in the mall.

Copper Leaf: Goan food/thali, amazing prawn curry.

Sangolda

Kismoor: Very popular with expat Goans for Goan food and live music nights with Tammy and Roy and other popular Goan duos and bands. Lots of ballroom dancing and jiving. It is the same with Altrude by the Sea in Candolim and Lazy Goose in Nerul.

Saligao

Cantare: Fantastic live music on many nights, a nice vibe and great drinks. There is lots of jiving as well.

The Second House: The latest trending place in town, it was opened in September 2023. I recognized it as my old friend Darryl's former house, which is big, bright and welcoming. Lots of old photos and interesting art. Attentive service. The ceviche and the vegan bibimbap bowl were both fresh and delicious.

Mr D'Souza's food truck outside Saligao's famous Mae de Deus church serves good choris pao and cutlet pao. Open only after 6 p.m., it gets sold out quickly.

Anjuna

Melt: Outdoors, good pizza.

Mahe: Outdoors, coastal, fusion, nice ambience. I loved the Mahua cocktail here. It shares its space with the charming Champaca bookstore, which also offers monthly book subscriptions and hosts launches and discussions.

Cream Choc: I am no expert but believe they are likely the best gelato in India. They also have outlets in Panjim and Porvorim.

Elephant & Co: A Pune export with good fusion food, fab cocktails and an inviting lavish location. Good live music and DJ. I enjoyed the chicken ghee roast tacos and the gin cocktails.

Posa@Artjuna: Sai has perfected her mindful gastronomy with a limited, curated and sustainable menu. The mackerel toast, ragi crackers and rainbows are my faves.

Slow Tide: Perfect Anjuna location with a classy beach shack ambience.

Assagao

Artjuna Bakery: Outdoor roadside café in Badem. Go early in the morning and have their croissants (almond for me). The pain au chocolat is recommended too.

Babka Goa: Café with good coffee, baked goods and fresh smoked salmon bagel sandwiches.

Mustard: Outdoors with great Bengali and French food. Also, live music.

Sublime: Old Goan house ambience and outstanding fusion food. The owner, Chris, is a gifted chef. Their many options of ceviche, carpaccio and tacos are all amazing.

Tamil Table: Great food and drinks, a nice place for fancy South Indian food.

Izumi: Outstanding Japanese food and drinks. Great vibe. Bigger and better than the original in Bandra. The sashimi and crab stick salad, the Hamachi truffle ponzu with wasabi jelly, and the mushroom and water chestnut gyozas are my go-to.

Assa House: Limited menu but decent French food. They sometimes have live music.

Morjim (beach)

Jardin D'ulysse Restaurant: Relaxing tree house ambience.

Burger Factory: Sprawling beachfront location with a vast range of burgers and attentive service.

Kuchun's: Delicious Indian fusion food (mostly Bengali), interesting cocktails, great hosts, service and sometimes, live music.

Rice Mill: Tiny place with cool coffee and cocktails. It is hopping on Saturday nights with live jazz.

Just 100 meters away is the truly stunning Morjai temple. The walls are stark white with the traditional now rare 'Kaavi' art friezes. Worth a visit.

Blue Turtle: Fabulous beach location, huge, plenty of parking, great selection of authentic Goan and other cuisines, and nice vibe.

Ashwem (beach)

La Plage: With fantastic French food, it's a classic. The tuna tartare and the chocolate thali are my favourites.

Amber Bar: Tiny, happening place for sundowners, playing our old-time 1970s classic rock kind of music.

Pagan Café/Babu Huts: A casual beach shack where you can spend the day swimming, eating, drinking and relaxing.

Mandrem (beach)

Lazy Dog: One of the fancier beach shacks to spend the day swimming, eating, drinking and relaxing.

Verandah: Lovely nouvelle cuisine and a secret gin bar.

Moira

7 Short 1 Long Restaurant: Good food, drinks and music. Belinda is an outstanding host. Do pop in, if you are around, for the vibe and her hospitality.

Nachinola

Eating at Andron is like eating at a friend's home. They offer all the Goan pork and beef classics, plenty of parking and good service. Their home-brewed masala feni is a must-try.

Ponda

Savoi Plantation: You can tour their extensive spice farms and taste the local produce in a delicious Goan meal, which brings a wide variety of interesting foods and flavours that you won't find elsewhere.

South Goa

This list is slim because I need to spend more time exploring this area, but we are working on it.

The Goan Kitchen in Margao did a great job delivering typical Goan Christmas sweet hampers to family and friends in Mumbai, Pune and Goa for Christmas 2021. With a small shop that does deliveries across Goa, they are trying to revive many of the traditional Goan sweets. They serve amazing Goan snacks and a set Goan lunch. They also offer a Loutolim lunch experience with an elaborate menu of Goan food and a bebinca-making demo. In order to dine here, bookings need to be made in advance.

Chef Avinash Martin's Cavantina and Table in the Hills offer outstanding nouvelle Goan food using seasonal ingredients with a twist.

Betty's place and Betty's boat cruises in Mobor provide boat trips on the Sal and good Goan food.

Kim's Fine Foods and her Around the Corner Bakery in Orlim have a selection of traditional Goan favourites that she cooks and bakes herself. She also curates a Goan food experience in her home with a selection of delicacies from starters to desserts.

Jila Bakery in Loutolim is famous for its melt-in-the-mouth eclairs. Like Kayani Bakery in Pune, it has a cult following. It is for insiders IYKYK* as there is no menu just a subtle name sign in an ancestral house.

Tejas on Talpona Beach has fresh fish and fish curry rice to go with the mesmerizing, pristine beach.

Surya and Santosh in Galgibaug offer fresh clams, crabs and oysters. They also do a mean prawn curry rice.

Here's my last list. Let me get on my soapbox and continue to preach.

When you live in Goa or visit, **please:**

- Be a responsible citizen of the planet and a responsible tourist/visitor.
- Stay calm, respectful and polite.
- Don't drink and drive. Don't drink till you pass out. Think about how you drive and where you pee.
- Remember your basic civic sense.
- Don't fight, bully, bargain, honk, shout and threaten.
- Think about the environment and how you dispose of every plastic or glass bottle, or packet you use once.
- Try to live beyond the beach and party stereotypes (beer, beach shack, eat, drink, party, repeat).
- Visit a heritage home, art gallery, church, temple or museum.
- Go on a walk—heritage or nature.
- Attend a film, arts or literary festival.

---

* Online slang for 'If you know you know'.

- Taste some local Goan food you have never tried before and/or try eating seasonal specials.
- Support local livelihoods with your tourist or expat rupee.

Let's work together for Goa to retain the charm we all came here for and not lose it to the capitalization of culture.

Epilogue

As I look ahead, I wonder what lies in store for Goa. Which Goa will exist for my children and their children?

Will it still be emerald and pristine with the open fields and the never-ending beaches? Will there be birdsongs and music?

Will it be bright lights, crowded casinos and super luxury towers like Vegas, a place that never sleeps?

Will those with their Portuguese passports or golden Dubai visas be long gone? Did the people who came here to find themselves, find themselves and move on? Will those who looked at Goa as an investment or the flavour of the year have found a new fancy and left? My main concern remains—what will happen to those sweet old ladies whom I pass every morning down my road sweeping their gardens? Or those kind old men who gather on that sankhov* and the benches facing the river every evening trying to solve the world's problems? They amble hesitantly, dodging the

---

* A low bench, a culvert.

Will the Siolim landscape look like this soon?

traffic and the potholes, fearing for their lives. Looking
wistfully where once were wide open spaces, at the fields
and fruit trees they lovingly cared for . . . Will they have
all become gentrified gated communities, luxury villas, and
golf courses?

Will the fields with complex rice crops, irrigation
systems and indigenous grains be covered with slums,
chawls, condos and swimming pools?

Will Chorão be underwater? Will river water rise to
reclaim some of the villages and will the hills collapse with
the hacking and overdevelopment?

I wonder if one day in the future, Goans will be like
the indigenous population in the new world whom we visit
through museums and curated experiences. I think about
the original inhabitants of lands who have been colonized—
Gawdas and Kunbis, Aboriginals, Maoris and the native
Americans/Canadians—whose reservations you visit, food
you taste, and customs and dances you watch, as a tourist
looking for some local history and culture. I can see the
possible future—the voyeuristic viewing of grand old Goan

houses with their sweeping verandahs, high ceilings, carved rosewood furniture, Belgian glass chandeliers and blue Macau pottery; Goans singing and playing fados, mandos and dulpods on their accordions, Portuguese guitars, violins and ghumots, or maybe jazz on the sax and alto sax, or rock and roll on the guitar, keyboard and drums; dancing the dekni, the mando, the kunbi or the jive and cooking Goan delicacies to entertain tourists who want to know what Goan living was.

How can we strike a balance? Live in a community where we care for each other, the environment and this great, small state? It is not just greed that motivates us but the wish for a better sustainable future and a better quality of life for everyone—the old, the young, the insiders, the outsiders, the Goans, locals, ex-pats, hippies, settlers, migrants, dogs, cows, pigs and even those monkeys . . .

I would like to end with this oft-quoted eloquent prose by Mumbai High Court Justice G. S. Patel in The Goa Foundation vs Ministry of Environment, Forest and Climate Change and the State of Goa, with which he won the hearts of Goans in October 2017:

This is an extraordinary state. In more ways than one, a place where, perhaps more than anywhere else, sky, sea and earth meet. From horizon to horizon, it is a land of abundant richness. It is a land of confluences, where diverse strands meet and co-exist; and, in a time of apparently incessant strife and discord, it is still a mostly liberal land. It is a kind and gentle land, of kind and gentle people. It is also a land that, given its small size and small population, has had a wholly disproportionate influence on our art, culture, language, music, literature, architecture, history, design and more (even food, for many of what we consider our staples first came from here). Its greatest asset is one: its environment and its ecology—its rivers and riverbanks, its beaches, its lakes and clear streams, its dense forests, its low hills and fertile fields, its boulders and even trees shrouded with moss and vines and lichen in the rains, its ridiculously brilliant sunsets. One needs only to turn off an arterial road to either east or west to see all this first-hand, and all of it within a few minutes . . . This is something no one can deny—this is a land truly worth fighting for.*

---

* Bar and Bench, http://images.assettype.com/barandbench/import/2017/
10/Goa-NGT-JUDGEMENT-watermark.pdf

Acknowledgements

I am eternally grateful to:

- My daughter, Divya, for her patient questioning, skilful negotiation and brutal editing. She, my husband, Bharat and my son, Kunal, had to listen to me all day, every day, as I hammered on about writing this book. All three are far better writers, readers and editors than I am. Kunal also took my author bio photos.
- My literary friends who read the rambling draft manuscript and gave their honest feedback—Arti Dwarkadas in Mumbai, India; Francine Giliomee in Stellenbosch, South Africa; Jackie LaPlante in Victoria, Canada; Gauri Kaushish in New Delhi, India; Teresa Turvey between Oxford, England, and Connecticut, USA; Vasu Balakrishnan in Kodaikanal, India and Abhay Puri, in Goa and Mumbai.
- Alexyz, for his Siolim support and the quintessential caricatures for the Siolim chapter.

- Rutuja, for the many detailed, unbelievable illustrations and Analise for the lovely line drawings of the cashew, garafao, ghumot and sausages.
- Legendary Goan writer Rajdeep Sardesai, for being so gracious with his time and thoughts and recommending my first book.
- Jerry Pinto, whose writing inspired me to find my Goan Catholic voice and celebrate it.
- The giants who read the chapters and gave feedback on the Goan context, including Norma Alvares, Tino de Sa, Celsa Pinto, Clifford DeSilva, Heta Pandit, Carlos Gracias and William Dias.
- My literary agency Jacaranda—Jayapriya Vasudevan for her professional heft, faith and encouragement, and Smita Khanna for her expertise. Harish Vasudevan for his poker face and outrageous humour.
- The editors at Penguin Random House India—Gurveen Chadha, Aparna Abhijit and Anushree Kaushal—and the team who helped edit, design, proofread, produce, print and publicize this book.
- Naresh Fernandes for introducing me to the world of publishing, listening to me agonize over the process and giving me many books that I needed to read.
- Frederick Noronha, for pushing me to find an international literary agent and publisher, for his commitment to recording and archiving Goa and for his Goa-centric WhatsApp groups that gave me ideas and insights into many things Goan.
- My neighbours, Maria, Tanya, Irene and Sally, helped with local references and lore. Sebastian D'Cruz, the

Siolim chronicler, for recording Siolim history, and his daughter, Jovera, for allowing me to recreate his map.

- Professional writers, editors and dear friends, Priya Mirchandani and Gayatri Kamath, who counselled me on my early draft proposals and my paralyzing self-doubt.
- Chetan Mahajan of the Himalayan Writing Retreat (HWR), and my cohort at the July 2022 creative writing course in Satkhol, Uttarakhand, especially Arun Muthu, who read draft chapters and kept reminding me 'show, don't tell'. The HWR virtual first draft club in July 2022 and April 2023 gave me a writing community.
- Outspoken journalist Vivek Menezes, who I followed on Facebook and learnt so much from.
- These greats who have written their own Goa stories— Lambert Mascarenhas, Maria Aurora Couto and Frank Simoes.
- Friends and family, who encouraged me to write a book after reading my blogs. Special thanks to my dear old Poona neighbour, Joey Coutinho, who greatly appreciated and widely circulated my 'Being Goan' blog in June 2020. He left us too soon in August 2020.
- My community of friends, family and colleagues across the world, who listened patiently and promised to buy the book.
- Reshma and Ajit, who manage most of the everyday running of my house, allowing me the freedom to sit for hours, days, weeks, and months to write this book.
- All the people I met, ran into, read and followed, and whose conversations I shamelessly eavesdropped on, for giving me these perceptions of Goa today.

- Everyone reading this, who generously gave their money and time to read my story. I hope it will resonate no matter where you come from, currently live, call home or are moving to.
- My parents, Albert and Biddie Mendonça, and to my grandparents Jerry and Lulu Mendonça, and Marshall and Eslinda D'Lima, for giving me Goa, my roots and belonging.